PRAISE FOR *GREAT LEADERSHIP*

"A must read for professionals from all sectors. The use of dynamic examples and easily understood models brings this often-times complex subject to life. This is a great primer for junior and senior leaders alike and easily converted into a meaningful and purposeful development program."

—**Lawson W. Magruder III, Lieutenant General, U.S. Army (retired)**

"A very readable and focused treatise on the essentials of leadership. Great Leadership very effectively makes the case for the critical role of character and competence in the making of great leaders. Bell has distilled the accumulated wisdom of our culture on the subject of great leadership so that we can learn as we practice and make the necessary adjustments along the way to avoid the very human tragedies that invariably happen when leadership fails."

—**Michael P. Kane, Senior Vice President, Holcim (US)**

"This book lays the foundation for great leadership and allows developing leaders to be exposed to the key elements of great leadership. It shows that with the right framework, ordinary people can become influential leaders. In this sense, it demonstrates that leaders are made, not born. People who start with this solid base are on their way to becoming great leaders."

—**Reid Dove, CEO, AAA Cooper Transportation**

"A must read for anyone even remotely interested in leadership today."

—**Al Walker, business consultant; author, *Thinking Big and Living Large*; past president, National Speakers Association**

GREAT LEADERSHIP

GREAT
LEADERSHIP

WHAT IT IS AND WHAT IT TAKES
IN A COMPLEX WORLD

ANTONY BELL

Davies-Black Publishing
Mountain View, California

Published by Davies-Black Publishing, a division of CPP, Inc. 1055 Joaquin Road, 2nd Floor, Mountain View, CA 94043; 800-624-1765.

Special discounts on bulk quantities of Davies-Black books are available to corporations, professional associations, and other organizations. For details, contact the Director of Marketing and Sales at Davies-Black Publishing: 650-691-9123; fax 650-623-9271.

Visit the Davies-Black Publishing Web site at www.daviesblack.com.

10 09 08 07 06   10 9 8 7 6 5 4 3 2 1
Printed in the United States of America

Library of Congress Cataloging-in-Publication Data

Bell, Antony
Great leadership : what it is and what it takes in a complex world / Antony Bell. — 1st ed.
    p. cm.
Includes index.
ISBN-13: 978-0-89106-215-8 (hardcover)
ISBN-10: 0-89106-215-7 (hardcover)
1. Leadership. I. Title.
HD57.7.B4476 2006
658.4'092—dc22

2006018795

FIRST EDITION
First printing 2006

For Betsy

CONTENTS

PART I
THE FOUNDATIONS FOR GREAT LEADERSHIP
Clarity from Confusion

PART II
CHARACTER IN LEADERSHIP
Soul, Heart, and Mind

PART III
COMPETENCE IN LEADERSHIP
Knowledge, Skill, and Talent

LIST OF FIGURES

LIST OF TABLES

PREFACE
A Different Look at Leadership

"Everything should be as simple as possible," Einstein once said, "and no simpler."

Leadership is complex. Most people wish it wasn't, but it is. Because it is, we tend to make it either too complicated to be manageable or too simple to be useful. Either way, we end up confused by the complexity or disillusioned by the simplicity. In all this confusion, we need to make sense of leadership so we can make great leadership attainable.

That's the ambition of this book. This is not another book that gives you three, five, or ten steps to great leadership. This book offers you a framework that will help you think and act your way to great leadership.

In our practice, we work with many gifted leaders. We also work with leaders who struggle. They all have one thing in common: they need a framework that clarifies what great leadership looks like—one that helps bad leaders become good, and good leaders become great.

Even the most gifted leaders need to understand how the different pieces of leadership fit together, so they know what kind of leadership to use in what conditions, whatever their level of responsibility. This book presents a comprehensive, manageable approach to leadership that gathers the different elements of great leadership into a coherent whole.

Most leaders are beyond formulas and sound bites. They are on a quest for real answers to the deeper questions of leadership. Leadership is a journey, and if the present terrain seems unstable and treacherous at times, the path ahead will seem even more uncertain. Leaders are looking for a map and a compass that give them a way of coping with the present and a way of preparing for the future.

This book is designed to be a companion for your journey, a map and compass to help you negotiate the terrain ahead. Its goal is to integrate all the critical components of leadership into a coherent model that is conceptually sound as well as intensely usable, that unifies all the fragmented viewpoints, theories, concepts, and notions about leadership—each of which is part of the story—into an easy-to-grasp, consolidated, workable approach. The purpose of this book is not only to help you apply great leadership to the challenges you face in your current role but also to help you figure out what you need to do to prepare for the leadership roles you anticipate on the path ahead.

Leadership is sometimes addressed in the same way the proverbial three blind men described an elephant: the one who felt the leg described the elephant as a tree trunk, the one who felt the tail described the elephant as a rope, and the one who felt the ear described the elephant as a huge leaf. None of them was wrong in his analogy; each was just incomplete. They all described pieces of the elephant.

This book describes the whole elephant. It allows you to figure out how the ear, the leg, and the tail fit with the rest of the elephant. It provides you with a workable framework that helps you make sense of every other leadership resource out there and helps you identify those that would be most useful to you.

And there is a bewildering supply of resources out there. The last time you felt challenged to strengthen your leadership skills, chances are you looked for a book. Which one did you pick? As you scrolled through Amazon.com or stood in front of the shelves at your local bookstore, you were confronted with books by a procession of academics, consultants, business leaders, military figures, politicians, and coaches competing for your attention. With this overload of often discordant information, if you persisted, you may have chosen in response to a book title, a cover, a recommendation, or maybe a crisis—rather than in response to something that meets the real needs and challenges you confront.

To guide and clarify that choice, you need a framework that allows you to see where all the past and present contributors fit into the big picture of leadership and organizational change—people like John Adair, Ichak Adizes, Warren Bennis, Ken Blanchard, Larry Bossidy, Marcus Buckingham, Ram Charan, Jim Collins, Stephen Covey, Peter Drucker, Tommy Franks, Daniel Goleman, Gary Hammel, Charles Handy, Paul Hersey, Barbara Kellerman, John Kotter, James Kouzes and Barry Posner, Rosabeth Moss Kanter, Patrick

Lencioni, Theodore Levitt, John Maxwell, Burt Nanus, Kenichi Omae, Tom Peters, Bill Pollard, Jerry Porras, Michael Porter, Colin Powell, Robert Quinn, Edgar Schein, Peter Scholtes, Peter Senge, Noel Tichy, Jack Welch, and many other worthy contributors I don't have room to cite.

With such a framework, you will not only see where these contributors fit, but their contributions will be all the more meaningful. Because you will know what you are looking for, you will pick the right responses and they will most likely meet or exceed your expectations. You won't expect them to deliver more than they can, and they may well deliver more than you expect.

So this book will help you

- *Distinguish the three dimensions of leadership and understand why applying them appropriately and fully is vital to well-led organizations.* I'll discuss these in greater depth later on, but for now it's enough to point out that the skills required for each dimension are very different, and each level of leadership responsibility requires a different mix of the three. In fact, much of the confusion over leadership is the confusion over these three dimensions.

- *Identify and understand the key elements of an organization that are critical for bringing about real change in it.* This analysis applies whether you have to deal with the organization in its entirety or just a piece of it. In these pages you will uncover the seven key elements of an organization and the relationships among them—making it easier to bring about the change you want to engineer.

- *Understand how character and competence influence each other.* Most of the emphasis in the workplace is on competence, but character is just as crucial to great leadership. You will discover a model that helps you understand the critical interplay between the two and how to create an environment where both are valued. And it will also help you figure out how your development as a leader will best be served.

The most effective way way to read this book is to start with Part I (discussing the foundations of leadership), and then choose either Part II (on character) or Part III (on competence), whichever appeals to you most. But, then, read the other.

And, as you read, think of this book as an invitation—an invitation to change the way people think about leadership and how they exercise it. It's also an invitation to teach leadership and pass it on, helping the people you lead pass it on to others in turn. It's an invitation to be a contagious carrier of great leadership.

Leaders and leadership have had a bad rep since the turn of this century, and with good cause; rarely have the levels of trust in our leaders been so low. Otherwise, perhaps we wouldn't read Dilbert with such relish.

With no ill-will to Scott Adams (Dilbert's creator), we'd all like to see the pointy-haired boss lose his preeminence as a symbol of marketplace leadership. We'd like to see our perceptions of leaders shaped less by the verdicts of courtroom juries and more by the well-placed trust of marketplace workers.

When leaders are transformed, the transformation of their organizations follows not far behind. This framework for great leadership works, and the timing is right. In the face of the extraordinarily complex environments leaders work in, there is a hunger for simple answers. That hunger has always been there; people have always wanted to improve their leadership skills. The difference now is that the hunger is coming not just from individual people but from organizations as well.

It's only recently that organizations have seen the critical importance of developing their leaders. In such a complex, competitive environment, many organizations have come to recognize, even if reluctantly, that the key to their success is their leadership, and the key to their competitive edge is great leadership. "Leadership is the single biggest constraint at Johnson & Johnson," J&J CEO Ralph Larsen once said, "and it is the most critical business issue we face."

The most significant thing about an organization, I often tell people, is what goes on in the minds of its leaders. (This is a phrase I first heard from my colleague Dan Wooldridge; when I asked him about its origin, he was too modest to claim it as his own, though I suspect it is.) The challenge you and I face is turning what goes on in those minds toward great leadership. As we seek to do that, may what follows help us spread the virus of great leadership. When it does, we may find that leadership that is as simple as possible and no simpler is not only attainable but also highly infectious.

ACKNOWLEDGMENTS

Any contribution of this kind stands on the shoulders of others; this book certainly does. Some are people I have never met, but their thinking and writing have stimulated and enriched my own. I have a deep appreciation for the research conducted by people like John Kotter, Jim Collins, Jerry Porras, and the Gallup Group. I owe these people much, and they may recognize their influence in these pages.

Others not only have influenced me but also have stretched me— the colleagues, clients, and friends who have pushed and challenged my thinking and practice and, in so doing, have strengthened and refined them. Dave Cornett, Greg Dawson, Bruce Jamieson, and Greg Wiens as partners became highly respected colleagues and deeply valued friends, as have others who walk the same path with me as colleagues and clients—people like Tom Alafat, Todd Cunningham, Reid Dove, Tom Fitzpatrick, Kelli Glasser, Kathy Hopkins, Mike Kane, Erik Hoekstra, Lawson Magruder, Ron Magnus, Leslie Martin, Matt Martin, Scott Peterson, Lindsley Ruth, Tom Schwartz, Dan Shoultz, Tim Spiker, Ed Walker, and Dan Wooldridge. In my more formative professional years, Paul Williams, Dean Truog, and John Ed Robertson offered me their time, wisdom, and friendship, which have been both an enduring gift and a powerful example. Earlier still, my father demonstrated qualities of leadership that I only later came to appreciate and recognize. I also greatly value the friendships I have formed with the NILD board members, and my association with friends and colleagues at FMI has been a very stimulating one. Eric Valentine did a masterful job in helping shape the proposal, and Mike Kane, John Kaneb, Pat Nolan, Dick Powell, Dan Shoultz, Al Walker, and Ed Walker also gave invaluable input and feedback on this book.

Connie Kallback, Jill Anderson-Wilson, and Laura Simonds at Davies-Black deserve special recognition—their support and careful, thoughtful editing and comments made them delightful to work with. They have my deepest appreciation.

My deepest gratitude goes to my wife, Betsy. Her encouragement, support, and feedback have been a powerful impetus, and the impact of her presence in the experiences that over the years have shaped the thoughts on these pages is incalculable. Dedicating this book to her doesn't do her justice.

And finally, as a man of faith, I would be remiss not to acknowledge my deepest gratitude to the One whose patience with me has been far greater than I have ever shown to those I have led.

PART I

THE FOUNDATIONS FOR GREAT LEADERSHIP

Clarity from Confusion

THE IMPORTANCE OF A LEADERSHIP FRAMEWORK

Understanding What's at Stake

Great careers are built on great leadership. At the end of your career—whether you retire as a CEO, a senior executive, a project manager, a department head, or a team leader, it makes no difference—you will be remembered by the quality of your leadership.

Not only will you be remembered by your leadership, but you will also judge yourself by it. If you could right now fast-forward to the conclusion of your career and look back at your leadership, you'd most likely focus on the major decisions that shaped your professional path—the Rubicons you crossed and the ones you didn't, the Alamos you fought and the ones you didn't. And you would be right to do so, because those decisions would all be significant—both the good choices and the poor choices that reflect great leadership and poor leadership.

And as you looked back over the decades, you would probably wish you had found a way to improve the consistency of those decisions—some kind of framework that would have helped you consistently practice great leadership.

Rewinding the tape back to the present, you can now look ahead with the confidence that such a framework does indeed exist. That's what this book is about—giving you the framework to make the choices for great leadership, so that when you get to the end of your career, you can look back over a consistent pattern of great leadership.

If you were to rewind the tape even further and look into the past before your own past, you would see that what is true for your personal history is true for the broad sweep of human history. You would see that the impact of history is the impact of leadership. At the fulcrum of momentous events and movements have stood personalities whose leadership tipped the balance for good or for evil. What would American independence have been without Adams, Franklin, Jefferson, or Washington? Or the Civil War without Lincoln? Or opposition to Hitler without Churchill? Or Indian independence without Gandhi? Or even Communism without Lenin or terrorism without bin Laden?

Some tipped the scales for good; some tipped it for bad. Many were inept, and their ineptitude made them memorable. Historian Barbara Tuchman devoted a book—*The March of Folly*—to what she called "wooden-headed leadership," which assesses "a situation in terms of preconceived fixed notions while ignoring or rejecting any contrary signs. It is acting according to wish while not allowing oneself to be deflected by the facts." Such leadership, she says, is "epitomized in a historian's statement about Philip II of Spain, the surpassing woodenhead of all sovereigns: 'No experience of the failure of his policy could shake his belief in its essential excellence.'"

THE COMPLEXITY OF LEADERSHIP

If great leadership was elusive in the past, it is even more so today. Consider these trends:

- *The expectations for business performance have never been so high on such a widespread scale.* The extraordinary economic growth that began in the 1980s and accelerated in the 1990s set expectations for business performance that are for the most part unsustainable, and—with a population increasingly engaged as investors—those expectations are no longer limited to institutional investors and market analysts.

■ *The level of scrutiny has never been so intense.* Scrutiny has never come from so many sources (sometimes simultaneously): the government (in all its many forms), the shareholders, the customers and their advocates, the employees, and the community. This scrutiny is beginning to keep some out of the race. The *Economist* quoted one chairman of a major publicly traded company as saying, "I spend my life advising friends of mine not to become chief executives of quoted companies, and by and large they take my advice." Those who don't take such advice don't stay in one place as long as their predecessors did—witness the accelerating turnover rate in CEOs triggered by the unmet expectations of demanding constituencies.

■ *The scope of business has never been so broad.* Many organizations operate in multiple countries, in multiple markets, and with multiple products. The tension between global expansion and local relevance has never been so acute. This is true whether or not you work for a globally active organization; even if your focus is your domestic market, you are subject to the trends and forces of globalization. Globalization is not a fad. It is a reality, and it's here to stay. The more the inevitable cross-exposure of different national and ethnic cultures shapes and defines local and global business interchange, the more organizations will depend on leaders who operate comfortably and intelligently in ethnically diverse and varied marketplaces.

■ *The pace of innovation has never been so rapid.* The Bureau of Labor Statistics estimated that the sum total of human knowledge doubled between 2000 and 2002, and this is in line with estimates suggesting that it doubled ten times between 1950 and 2000. Doubling, by the way, is exponential: doubling ten times (1, 2, 4, 8, 16, and so on) actually means human knowledge was 1,024 times greater. In contrast, knowledge doubled only once between 1900 and 1950.

■ *The structures of organizations have never been so complex.* The sheer size of organizations today itself complicates the task of leading them. Much of their growth has come from acquisitions, so to the challenge of coping with size has been added the challenge of blending cultures. The *Wall Street Journal* observed that the average annual revenue of the fifty largest public companies in the United States was 70 percent higher by the end of the 1990s than it was in 1984. In the mid-1980s, eighteen companies employed more than 100,000 people; by the end of the 1990s, that number was over fifty. For such organizations, choices are multiple and complex, and with every acquisition and every joint venture or alliance another layer of complexity is added. With the recession at the dawn of the twenty-first century the pace slowed, but it didn't take long to pick up again.

■ *The span of control has never been so broad.* Corporate demographics have changed, particularly in terms of reporting structures. With the continual erosion of middle management over the past fifteen years, more and more people report to fewer and fewer leaders. The paradoxical consequence is that leaders have more responsibility, but they have less time to think about how to fulfill that responsibility.

■ *The confidence of the public in corporate leadership has never been so low.* We've seen plenty of cases of corporate leaders enriching themselves at the expense of their employees, and the sense of betrayal is all the greater because of the increased social role corporations play in today's society—for many people, their work is the only place they experience anything close to a sense of community. When leaders defraud a corporation, they betray the community that appointed them as guardians of that community; the betrayal is social as much as economic.

■ *The honeymoon for a new CEO has never been so brief.* Time is not on the side of business leaders: there isn't much room for mistakes, and there isn't time to grow.

THE COMPETITIVE ADVANTAGE OF GREAT LEADERSHIP

With all these challenges, it stands to reason that any organization that provides the leadership to overcome them has a huge competitive advantage. These challenges don't mean that great leadership is impossible; in fact, great challenges have a way of uncovering great leaders. "I am apt to think," Abigail Adams once wrote in a letter to her husband, commenting on George Washington, "that our late misfortunes have called out the hidden excellencies of our commander-in-chief," and quoting English poet Edward Young, she added, "Affliction is a good man's shining time." No less so today, despite many examples of poor leadership; some leaders still prove capable of rising, under pressure, to the levels of greatness their organization needs. And fortunately so, because no single factor shapes the results of an organization more than the kind of leaders it raises and recruits.

The leadership an organization embraces ultimately determines the results it generates. "In the old days, I would have said it was capital, history, the name of the bank," John Reed once said when he was running Citicorp. "Garbage—it's about the guy at the top." Many organizations claim that their people are their greatest asset, but that's not so, even for those that genuinely believe it (few do). An organization's leaders are its greatest asset, and an organization that takes care of its leaders takes care of every other asset, including its people.

Research bears this out. Great leadership was one of the critical ingredients in Jim Collins's research for *Good to Great*—it was in fact the first critical ingredient in the transformation of average companies into great companies. A recent MIT study gave further empirical support to the intuitively obvious fact that similar companies led by different leadership styles produce very different results. In strategy alone, for example, some focused on organic growth and others on growth by acquisition; some held more cash and others more debt (the latter in both cases did less well). The differences in style and strategy led to very different results in performance and profitability.

Not only is the impact of great leadership felt at an organizational level, it is also felt at an individual level. Leaders who know how to evoke talent stand out, and they deliver dramatic results, as demonstrated by Gallup's research in *First, Break All the Rules,* where extraordinary individual performance is attributed to the critical role of leaders who know how to bring out the best in the people they lead.

Not surprisingly, the importance of leadership is increasingly a matter of perception as well as fact. Consulting company Burson-Marsteller tracks such perceptions by measuring the impact of the CEO on the company's overall reputation, and from 1997 to 2003, it went from 40 percent to 50 percent. However effervescent or self-effacing the CEO, that one individual disproportionately but decisively shapes the perception of the company.

FIGURE 1. THE BOTTOM-LINE IMPACT OF GREAT LEADERSHIP

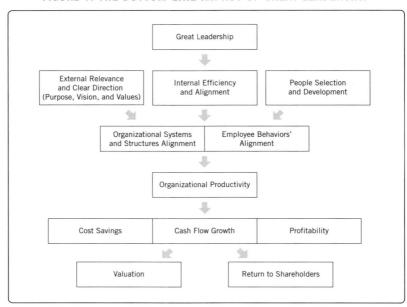

Of course, great leadership plays all the way down to the bottom line, as illustrated in Figure 1. When great leadership is exercised in its three main dimensions—external relevance, internal efficiency, and people selection and development—employee behaviors and their alignment with the organization's direction inevitably raise the level of the organization's productivity. When the organization's productivity is raised, costs are contained, cash flow grows, and profits build—boosting the valuation of the organization and the shareholder returns it generates.

All told, not a bad return for investing your organization with great leadership.

HOW LEADERS HANDICAP THEMSELVES

For all the importance of great leadership, it doesn't happen by itself. Without a framework, leaders often handicap themselves in a number of significant ways:

- *Leaders tend to operate from intuition and experience.* While both can serve a leader well, neither is infallible: intuition cannot compensate for the blind spots every person has, and experience is a tutor with a limited perspective.

- *Leaders tend to become leaders because they are technically competent.* Being good at something singles them out for promotion. But what makes people effective at one level can make them ineffective at another.

- *Leaders tend to operate with the skills that were most useful two levels below their current level.* In part because of the way they were chosen for the leadership track, they tend to maintain the mind-set of the level where they last felt real mastery.

- *Few leaders are taught to lead.* Because most leaders learn intuitively from experience, that experience is seldom analyzed with any depth, consistency, or systematic feedback. A few leaders have the good fortune of being taught informally by a particularly effective boss or mentor, but such teachers are rare. Even fewer leaders are taught formally; academic institutions focus on the organization of work more than on the application of leadership. MBA programs don't teach leadership, or, at best, they teach only a narrow portion of it. Many corporations offer in-house programs, but few combine strong teaching with the kind of in-depth coaching that guarantees its application.

- *Leaders tend to stop learning in midlife.* By the time people hit their forties, many rely on their previous knowledge and have only a shallow commitment to ongoing self-education and self-development.

- *Few leaders lead from a clear sense of purpose.* Even fewer lead from a clear sense of noble purpose.

- *Few leaders know how to pass on what they know.* Not having been taught, they have little idea how to help others develop their leadership skills.

To overcome these obstacles, leaders need some guidelines; they need a framework for understanding and exercising great leadership.

SOME LEADERSHIP REALITIES

- People are not an organization's greatest asset. Leaders are. If you invest in your leaders, you'll take care of every other asset—including your people.

- Leaders define their organization. What they think and how they think is crucial to the organization's success; what goes on inside their minds has greater impact on the organization than any other single factor.

- Organizations don't achieve greatness without planning for it, without consciously applying the principles that lead to greatness. Applying those principles is a leadership function.

- To guide their thinking about the organization and its growth and transformation, leaders don't need a program, but they do need a framework. Individual giftedness and intuition are seldom enough; in fact, they can be a handicap, because giftedness and intuition can keep leaders from uncovering their blind spots.

- Organization development and leader development need to be addressed together. The two are inseparably intertwined. You cannot change an organization without developing its leaders (at all levels of the organization).

- Leaders need to understand how the three dimensions of leadership apply to their particular role. Ignorance or misunderstanding of these three dimensions is among the main reasons for a leader's frustration or ultimate derailment.

- Organizations are best led when the right kind of leadership is intentionally and systematically applied to the right context and at the right level. Errors in this area cause much of the confusion in leadership.

WHY YOU NEED A FRAMEWORK

Several years ago, my wife and children surprised me with a gift of six tennis lessons for Father's Day. Though I'd been a respectable recreational tennis player for many years, I had mused from time to time about my need for some instruction—I knew I was doing some things wrong, but I didn't know what or why. Their gift was designed to silence my musings.

The lessons were eye-opening: I discovered that the force of the return came not from the strength of my arm, but (counterintuitively) from the power of my legs as I straightened my flexed knees to bring the full weight of my body into the return swing, sending the unsuspecting ball back with a force and accuracy that hitherto had been a matter of happenstance. I learned the value of the two-handed backhand, and I discovered that even the way I crossed the court influenced the quality of my return.

I learned that you don't have to be the best to compete; you just have to train better than the rest. And to train better than the rest, you have to know how to train. That's what my instructor did: he showed me how to train and gave me a strategy, a framework for my improvement. It was liberating. I might not be able to beat a Sampras or an Agassi, but now my game could go to a level it had never reached before.

So it is with leadership. We need the right knowledge to shape and mold our talent, and we need a strategy to develop it. We need a framework that helps us understand what great leadership looks like and develops our talent. Your innate talent for leadership isn't enough. Innate talent needs a framework for development—most upcoming leaders are in a position much like that of gifted high school football players in the United States, who need the framework provided by their college sports experience to survive in the National Football League.

Leaders stand or fall not so much by their talent or lack of it as by their understanding or misunderstanding of what great leadership is. That's why leaders need a framework. If you build your leadership from an integrated framework, the quality of the leadership within your organization will be immeasurably enhanced—however large or small your organization and whatever your level of experience. Here's what a framework will do for you:

1. *Your leadership talent will be strengthened and enriched because it will be fed with the right knowledge.*

   Talent is never enough. Much of leadership is counterintuitive, and at some point, intuition and experience either will mislead you or won't apply.

2. *You will develop and strengthen your own set of convictions and principles about leadership.*

   This approach gives you practical tools that help you distinguish the three fundamental (and fundamentally different) kinds of leadership and provides you with a framework to know when and how to exercise them.

This approach also gives you a framework to think deeply about the way you lead and what drives your leadership style. Your leadership style will be driven more by principle than by technique. Technique is important, but without principle, technique becomes manipulation. Effective leaders operate from a clear set of principles and a leadership philosophy that give coherence to their leadership style.

This is no new concept. Plato argued long ago, "The philosophers must become kings in our cities or those who are now kings and potentates must learn to seek wisdom like true philosophers, and so political power and intellectual wisdom will be joined in one." Without leaders becoming thinkers, he warned, "there can be no rest from the troubles for the cities, and I think for the whole human race." That holds true for twenty-first-century corporations.

John Wooden is considered one of the most outstanding basketball coaches in the history of the game. His success, however, came not from the techniques he practiced as a coach but from the philosophy of leadership and success that he developed over time. He spent fourteen years shaping and defining it, but once he was satisfied with it—he eventually identified seventeen components of success and organized them in his now-famous pyramid—he applied it systematically, with the kind of results that justly earned him the accolades very few in his profession have enjoyed.

Wooden's philosophy of leadership and his definition of success ("the peace of mind obtained only through the self-satisfaction of knowing that you made the effort to do the best of which you are capable") stand in stark contrast to the usual definition of success ("winning isn't everything—it's the only thing"). It's this conscious definition and execution of a philosophy of success and leadership that allowed Wooden to transcend his peers. Leaders can take their cue from him: leaders who transcend their peers are those who define and refine their leadership philosophy and then apply it systematically, rather than succumbing to leadership defined by the latest slogan.

For John Wooden, defining his philosophy of success and how he would lead others to live it was at the heart of his effectiveness and greatness as a coach and as a leader. In the same way, this approach helps you lay the foundations for outstanding leadership, not only in the exercise of your role but also throughout your whole organization. You will see how greatness cannot be achieved without competence and how it cannot be sustained without character.

3. *You will understand organizations in a new way—especially your organization.*

Earlier, I mentioned the limitations of intuition and experience for a leader's development. These factors are equally limiting for understanding organizations, because intuition and experience typically don't detect the internal and external forces that undermine the purpose and direction the leaders have set for the organization. A framework, however, offers a clear picture of the interweaving dynamics of the organization and guards leaders from the blind spots that otherwise inevitably keep them from addressing critical organizational issues. Such a framework also removes the mystery from the complexities of organization design and renewal.

By the same token, none of the critical elements of organizational change will be overlooked, and these critical elements will all come together in a coherent whole. You will avoid a haphazard and piecemeal approach, and you will sidestep the pitfalls of one-dimensional programs with five, seven, or ten steps; instead, the framework will give you the structure to determine critical change priorities.

Organizational change and renewal is a journey, with its own allotment of rough terrain and inclement weather, and this approach provides you with a map and a compass so that you don't lose hope in the desert or go astray in the fog. The map and compass will steer you through the pitfalls of your organization's transformation, and you won't be blindsided by the unseen forces of organizational resistance.

4. *At a time when the pressures of leading and managing change are unparalleled, you will lead with greater focus and clarity.*

The overwhelming speed of change today requires leaders to operate not only as good executors but also as good anticipators—leaders who can keep one step ahead of the changes. No wonder Andy Grove, CEO of Intel, wrote a book called *Only the*

Paranoid Survive. The challenge for corporate leaders is huge; in this changing landscape, the very nature of corporate leadership is changing. Organizations are increasingly complex and choices more difficult, and in such an environment leaders need to be able to know what to keep and what to change, a distinction more easily made with the right kind of framework. It won't be only the paranoid who survive; the well-guided and the well-resourced will be among the survivors.

5. *You will clarify your leadership message.*

Leaders typically underestimate what it takes to clarify and transmit their message. Few leaders give the thought, time, and energy to sharpening their message, and, worse still, they underestimate the amount of airtime their leadership message needs. This approach helps you become the master broadcaster of your leadership message.

6. *You will stack the odds of success for your strategy of growth and transformation heavily in your favor because you will integrate leader development with organization development.*

Organization growth and transformation is a tricky business, but the framework for your development as a leader and for the growth and transformation of your organization makes sure you address what needs to be addressed at the time it needs to be addressed. And the thoroughness of a systematic approach increases your likelihood of implementing your growth and transformation strategies cost-effectively and promptly.

7. *You will learn a methodology that you can apply to any corporate environment.*

Learned methodologies have ongoing and multiple applications. The intense pressure to perform, the hunger for answers, and the disappointment in many of the answers encountered in the past have bred a caste of cynics and skeptics who have tried successive solutions that failed to deliver the supercharged performance they were anticipating. This framework is designed to help you win over the cynics because it is a methodology, not a program, and as such can be applied to virtually any corporate environment.

8. *You will make sense of the extraordinary volume of business literature.*

Business books are a booming business—proof, if proof were needed, of the extraordinary hunger for answers in leading, changing, and redefining organizations. As many have pointed out, we do not live in the Information Age, we live in the Information Overload Age. Without a means of evaluating this overload of business information, most leaders either read haphazardly or don't read at all. When they read, it tends to be reactively rather than in a concerted effort to address their real needs and challenges. This approach avoids such reactive reading.

9. *You will have a framework for personal growth and learning.*

Henry Kissinger once remarked that new administrations rely on knowledge and learning they possessed before they moved into office, and, once there, they seldom learn and grow. I have noticed a similar phenomenon: most business leaders stop learning in their forties.

This framework counters learning atrophy. More than just a methodology of leading change, this is also an approach to learning. It allows you to make sense of every resource you come across and every book you read (or are told to read). You will see how each solution fits into the overall process of change. You won't be bouncing from one solution to another driven by the latest best-seller or the recommendations of a colleague; you will be able to identify those that genuinely serve your interests.

10. *You may very possibly save your career.*

Talent doesn't guarantee success. Leaders, however gifted, often derail because they don't understand the critical levers of their organization. They also don't understand the essential elements of leadership, and because they don't, they misapply them. You can avoid these career killers.

MONUMENTS AND FOOTPRINTS

William Faulkner once made a distinction between monuments and footprints. We build monuments to commemorate great achievements, but footprints, he argued, are far superior: monuments tell us we got so far and no farther; footprints tell us we kept on moving.

This book is about footprints, not monuments. It offers a framework to help you define the direction of your footprints and provides you with a compass to get you to your goal. It will clarify leadership for those who practice it and for those who aspire to more of it. It seeks to provide leaders with a deeper, clearer understanding of the organizations they lead and the different kinds of leadership their organizations need. It also seeks to help leaders think differently and deeply about their roles as leaders.

You may have plenty of monuments to your name, but, in today's corporate environment, monuments are fragile and short-lived, quickly erected and quickly forgotten. With the intense pressure for high performance from the marketplace, the boardroom, or the big board (or from all three), there is little patience for footprints that endlessly circle the last monument.

With a focus on footprints, there is almost no limit to the difference your leadership can make to your organization and to those directly or indirectly touched by it. You will not only shape your environment to reach the aspirations of your organization, you will also create the environment that brings out the best in your people. You will be making footprints others will want to follow, and you will leave the task of building monuments to others. They may even build them to you.

2

THE SOURCE OF OUR CONFUSION

Understanding and Resolving the Complexity of Leadership

"Almost everyone in this country, I expect, would like to be thinner," author and journalist David Halberstam once commented. "And even more than thinner, I suspect that everyone would like to be a leader." True enough, but such aspirations for leadership face highly complex conditions: we live in a complex world, we compete in complex marketplaces, and we lead in complex organizations. As the complexity of leadership has grown over the past twenty-five years, so has the volume of literature addressing it, with an unabated outpouring from practitioners and academics alike. Much of that literature is confusing, and, to eliminate the confusion and unravel the complexity, it's necessary to start by understanding the origins and evolution of the demands on leadership through recent history to the present day.

THE PILGRIMS AND THE FOUNDING FATHERS

America was founded by a small group of tough-minded and determined men and women, who at great cost and great risk left all to carve out a society defined by their religious and political convictions. They and the generations that followed them endured hardships that soon became part of American folklore, as they built a society that eventually earned its independence. Their legacy has done much to shape our perceptions of leadership, even though they operated in a society far more homogeneous than our own: they were defined by a common set of values with a common code of conduct, based mostly on broadly held and deeply ingrained Judeo-Christian beliefs. Even if the theological foundations of these beliefs were not universally embraced, the code of conduct based on them was.

These early leaders gave considerable thought to—and engaged in intense debate about—the kind of structures that would reflect the way they wanted to organize their world, thus laying the foundations for what George Washington was to call the "Great Experiment"--the deliberate and intentional creation of a nation founded on a set of principles and ideas, or, as John Adams put it, "a government of laws and not of men." This was a striking departure from prior human experience where nations had evolved, not from an idea, but from the blurred history of almost untraceable geographic and migratory origins.

As the American colonies evolved and matured, the inability of the British ruling classes to recognize their evolution ultimately led to the American Revolution. The fight for American independence was no accident or historical aberration; it followed the natural logic of the values brought over by the Pilgrim Fathers. John Adams claimed that the Revolution was started in the minds of Americans long before the first shots were fired at Lexington and Concord and long before the first signature was penned on the Declaration of Independence. The epitaph on his tombstone is telling:

> This stone and several others have been placed in this yard by a great, great, grandson from a veneration of the piety, humility, simplicity, prudence, frugality, industry and perseverance of his ancestors in hopes of recommending an affirmation of their virtues to their posterity.

Adams chose "to say nothing [on his tombstone] of any of his own attainments," as David McCullough points out in his biography of John Adams, "but rather to place himself as part of a continuum, and to evoke those qualities of character that he had been raised on and that he had striven for so long to uphold."

The Great Experiment was thus a very deliberate attempt to shape society and to shape it around a set of values. Adams, Jefferson, Franklin, and Madison plundered history, literature, and political theorists—Adams alone examined over fifty sources—to uncover the secrets of the rise and fall of great empires and modern democracies. And they evidently succeeded. The extraordinary achievement of the American Revolution was not so much in getting rid of the oppressors (the French and Russian revolutions did that—with a great deal more bloodshed), but in creating and building a nation founded on solid principles and noble ideals, embedded in a legal framework that protected those principles and ideals (something the French and Russian revolutions did not do).

THE LEADERSHIP LEGACY OF THE FOUNDING FATHERS

Leadership, then, was defined by service. You served by leading, and because leadership was an act of service—political leaders were "public servants"—leadership was honored and respected, and so were the titles that went with a leadership role—titles that were earned, not inherited. The Duke of Bedford once quipped that in England he was respected because he was the thirteenth Duke of Bedford; in America, he would have been respected had he been the first. Because authority was honored, roles were unambiguous, and there was no confusion in gender roles, generational roles, or professional roles. Age and seniority were respected, and loyalty was prized. So was hard work; the work ethic—the so-called Protestant work ethic—taught that if you worked hard, you would be rewarded, if not now, then later.

These values shaped America for a long time; everything in society reinforced these perceptions of authority and leadership. The family (the primary repository of social and moral values) reinforced them, as did schools and neighbors. So did the church; the majority went to church and heard basically the same sermons. They may not have embraced the tenets of Christianity, but they never fundamentally challenged the code of conduct that flowed from them. These values shaped the common response to authority, the way people governed themselves, the political and legal infrastructures they established, and ultimately the constitution they wrote.

These values also shaped the way business was conducted. Knowledge and information were closely held by the leaders at the top, and they controlled the financial information. They maintained the closest ties to the customers, conducted the marketing, shaped the working conditions, and made the strategic decisions.

While many leaders today may long for a return to such a time, the social structures that allowed such leadership perceptions to flourish are gone and have been gone for a long time. So what has changed? And how have these changes affected the challenges leaders face today?

THE RISE OF LARGE ORGANIZATIONS

The dawn of the twentieth century was a critical turning point. As the century began unfolding, the United States edged its way onto the world stage, unheralded but aggressively nonetheless. By 1912, U.S. steel production outstripped that of Germany, making the United States the world's largest producer of steel. It wasn't recognized at the time, but early in the century, the United States became the world's most powerful economy.

For the first time, that economy was driven by very large corporations. A new economic phenomenon emerged: companies that marshaled more people than many national military forces, reshaping not only the economic landscape but also the life and conduct of the organization. With such huge organizations, control of information became blurred; who, for example, now had the best handle on the financial information? Who was in tune with the customer? Who knew the needs of the workforce? Who had control and access to the critical information? It wasn't the people at the top anymore; it was the people in the middle. The traditional structures of leadership no longer applied to such organizations.

With large organizations dominating the economy, the workplace became more complex. The challenge was making this complexity work, and the challenge gave birth to a new term: management. The focus became operational—keeping up with the increasing complexity of these organizations in a rapidly growing mass-manufacturing economy. The complexity of business organizations caught the attention of sociologists such as Max Weber and Henri Fayol. Weber focused on the study of bureaucracy and Fayol on the management of

French mines; Fayol was in fact the first to lay out a set of management principles. In the United States, the earliest pioneers were Henry Ford and Alfred P. Sloan, both pragmatists to the core, as you would expect. The need was for a highly operational focus, and management filled the need.

As I trace this history of leadership perceptions, keep in mind that *management* and *operational leadership* are synonymous terms.

Management as the Cornerstone of American Business

Management as a business concept reached full-blown maturity in the second half of the century. Its explosive growth was fueled by the complex challenges of massive modern warfare in World War II and by the powerful postwar economic forces the war unleashed—both of which gave tremendous impetus to the science of management. The workforce changed, too, with the influx of women replacing the men fighting the war, further complicated by the phenomenal growth in technological innovation, starting slowly in the 1950s and reaching exponential proportions by the 1980s. In the process, business thinking became solidly cemented in a very management—in a very operational—mind-set.

The Handicap of a Management Focus

In the decades that followed World War II, the huge U.S. domestic market was at first an asset, and then it became a liability. American companies operated in a large, homogeneous, and familiar domestic market, allowing them to grow to the size of multinational corporations without becoming genuinely multinational. While American companies could focus on tactical growth because of the size and nature of their domestic market, European and Japanese companies had no such luxury, forcing them to look at growth in much more strategic terms. Growth in the United States was thus possible with operational rather than strategic leadership, and, after World War II, corporate leaders made the classic mistake of working *in* the business rather than *on* the business. Because of the immense complexity of running these organizations, the focus became managing them rather than positioning them.

The legacy of management has been so deeply ingrained that it remains with us today; we cannot conceive of business practice without it. It shapes the curriculum of virtually every MBA program developed over the past thirty years and has propelled these programs' immense (though waning) popularity, training people in operational and financial leadership rather than in organizational and strategic leadership. America's pragmatic how-to culture found management's operational focus appealing, and its highly quantifiable and measurable approach could reduce almost every industry and business sector to the sum of its project management initiatives.

Management, however, is a methodology, not a set of values. It is neutral; what you do with management is what matters. A focus on operational efficiency is critical to an organization; but, just as people cannot live by bread alone, so organizations cannot live by management alone. Great management can produce an Eichmann managing the gas chambers, but it can't produce a Washington or a Jefferson managing a new nation. Had they simply been great managers, there might never have been an American Revolution.

In some ways they *were* great managers, of course, but they were above all great visionaries. "In everything, one must consider the end," John Adams would say, quoting Jean de la Fontaine, and the end they considered lay far beyond their own lifetimes. They were also men of tremendous strength of character. Benjamin Rush, one of the signers of the Declaration of Independence, said of John Adams that he was "equally fearless of men and the consequences of a bold assertion of his opinion." These men were anchored in the universal virtues of principle, courage, and hard work.

With the new emphasis on management in the second half of the twentieth century, the emphasis on character in leadership began to weaken, and the focus in leadership went from being the right kind of person with the right kind of character to a focus on developing the right kind of skills with the right kind of techniques.

The answer is not to eliminate management but to support it. Management is a one-dimensional perspective of leadership, and leadership is three-dimensional: leadership is exercised with an organization, with a task or operation, and with people, which is why it is possible to talk of *organizational leadership* (focused on the relevance of the organization in the larger marketplace), *operational leadership* (focused on the efficiency of internal operations), and *people leadership* (focused on bringing out the best in the people who work there). Organizations need to be led, tasks and operations need to be led, and people need to be led, and in each case the leadership skills are different. Management provided excellent operational leadership but no organizational or people leadership. From the 1980s on, then, we witnessed a strong reaction to management and some strong voices speaking for the other two dimensions—but not before a wake-up call in the 1970s.

THE JAPANESE JUGGERNAUT AND THE CHALLENGE TO LEADERSHIP PARADIGMS

While American companies were focusing on the internal mechanisms of their own companies, Japanese companies led by the likes of Sony were eyeing the world's markets and were steadily rebuilding themselves into a formidable competitive force. Taught by W. Edwards Deming and Joseph Juran and their disciples (rejected prophets in their own country but enthusiastically embraced by the Japanese), Japanese managers became the engineers of a management transformation, driven by a competitive passion for efficiency that took management to a new level, eventually dispelling the image of poor-quality products and services and facilitating the unprecedented invasion that hit U.S. markets in the 1970s.

The Japanese juggernaut was a shock for American companies, and, in an effort to explain its impact, they scrutinized Japanese business practices through the management lens of what had become slow and pedantic bureaucracies. What they saw through this lens was management finely tuned and fiercely applied. Unfortunately, they drew the wrong conclusions: what they failed to see was the discipline of strategic intent.

Because management had become the primary lens for assessing and measuring business performance, American business leaders' perception of the Japanese model simply reinforced their commitment to management. Ascribing the impact of the Japanese phenomenon to fine-tuned management was an unfortunate conclusion, because it only partially explained their success. The Japanese had also been very strategic in their penetration of the U.S. markets, but that was missed (even though it was well captured by authors such as Kenichi Omae, a Japanese business consultant who wrote *The Mind of the Strategist,* first published in 1981); instead, it was Japanese management practices that caught the attention of American leadership.

THE TUMULTUOUS EIGHTIES: ORGANIZATIONAL LEADERSHIP AND PEOPLE LEADERSHIP VERSUS OPERATIONAL LEADERSHIP

The early 1980s were watershed years. They ushered in a much murkier view of leadership, largely because of a widespread sense of what wasn't wanted (more focus on management, or operational leadership) coupled with little sense of what was. The hunger for a new kind of leadership came on the heels of an unappetizing diet of discredited and uninspiring leadership during much of the 1970s. Politically, Nixon's leadership was discredited, Carter's was uninspiring, and both opened the door to Ronald Reagan's visionary leadership, which swept him into office. The same trend was mirrored in the business community, where a new breed of leaders, characterized by the likes of Lee Iacocca and Jack Welch in the traditional economy and Steve Jobs and Bill Gates in the new economy, offered a different kind of leadership with compelling visions for their industries.

Two broad trends emerged: an *organizational* leadership focus and a *people* leadership focus, both in reaction to the earlier focus on operational leadership. The first addressed the organizational dimension with an emphasis on visionary leadership—the ability to create a compelling vision, and the qualities you need to inspire commitment to that compelling vision. The second addressed the people dimension of leadership—the ability to bring out the best in the people working for you. Figure 2 charts the evolution of leadership over the 1980s and 1990s.

The first trend—a focus on organizational leadership (leading the organization in such a way that it remained externally relevant)— made much of the distinction between leaders and managers, where a leader sets the vision and the manager executes the vision. But the distinction has carried unfortunate emotional overtones: some observers defined leaders as "doing the right thing" and managers as "doing things right"—a distinction that doesn't validate managers; doing things right doesn't help if you are not doing the right thing. The implication is obvious: be a leader, not a manager, because managers aren't doing the right thing.

This emphasis was reinforced in the early 1980s by authors such as Bert Nanus and Warren Bennis, who described America as "over-managed and under-led." And they were right; they had captured the

FIGURE 2. THE INCREASED COMPLEXITY OF LEADERSHIP

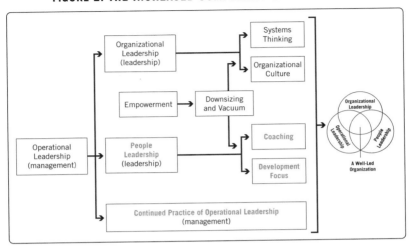

essence of leadership in the 1970s. The great value of this new emphasis on organizational leadership was in forcing leaders to think outside the organization and to see their companies in a far broader context. But one side effect was a strong reaction against the whole notion of management, which became the ugly stepsister.

Out of this organizational focus—either as a cause or a product, or possibly both—came the boom in the consulting industry. The ferment of ideas was ideal fertilizer for companies that offered solutions and road maps in the now confusing world of organizational growth. At the head of the pack was McKinsey, with firms like the Boston Consulting Group and Bain and Co. not far behind. Some, such as Gemini, took a message of wholesale organizational transformation to their clients. As the information-technology economy gathered momentum in the early 1980s, other consulting firms, such as Andersen Consulting (later Accenture), took a narrower technological perspective of organizational change. Behind the big names came a slew of lesser ones, some academics turned consultants, some practitioners in their own right.

The second trend—the focus on people leadership—was also a reaction to the uninspiring management mentality of the 1950s to 1970s: it's not visionary leadership you need, so went the argument, but leadership that gives you a motivated, energetic, and empowered workforce. The key is what you do at an individual level, not at an organizational level.

This focus spawned the growing emphasis on personal development, with the notion of personal ownership (rather than corporate ownership) for career development. Tom Peters, Paul Hersey, and Ken Blanchard were some of the early spokesmen, and the movement was reinforced by the proliferation of public seminars and the birth of a sophisticated seminar and business education sector.

Both tracks converged on empowerment as a major theme of the 1980s. For visionary or organizational leadership, an empowered workforce was the prerequisite for achieving the company's strategic imperatives. For the people-development emphasis in leadership, empowerment was the grassroots rallying cry for personal productivity. Tom Peters and others popularized the notion, and empowerment became a catchword.

Also behind the thrust for empowerment was the transition of an economy now powered by information technology rather than by mass manufacturing. The workforce that drove this economy was no longer the supposedly mindless labor force of mass manufacturing; the information-technology economy was now fueled by an army of "knowledge workers," an expression first coined by Peter Drucker. Knowledge workers, it soon became evident, wanted to be empowered.

The common analogy was the orchestra, the ultimate in flat organizations, where one leader (the conductor) coordinated the efforts of numerous performers. An apt analogy in the right context, it overlooked the fact that such organizations require skilled, competent, and self-motivated employees; orchestras function only with musicians who know how to play, want to improve, and want to perform at their highest level. Orchestra members don't need basic training in their core skills; they need coordinating.

Empowerment also produced some unanticipated consequences. In the logic of empowerment, middle management became redundant: if you have an empowered workforce, you don't need middle managers. The revolutionary zeal of empowerment took many to the guillotine, and in the wave of downsizings that hit the late 1980s and the early 1990s, the heads that rolled belonged mostly to middle management (a novelty in downsizing trends). The logic of empowerment was a flatter, more responsive organization, unencumbered by unnecessary layers of management; while it was pursued in some cases as a cynical cloak for cost cutting, it was mostly pursued in the misplaced faith that the very act of de-layering would usher in a new era of empowerment. The net result in most cases was that the people who were supposed to be empowered had no real sense of what it meant to be empowered. Empowerment often generated more frustration than freedom. A battered workforce had by this time seen just about everything in terms of change programs, and some took their stand as the last of the BOHICAs—"Bend over, here is change again." Instead of being entrusted with responsibility, they became encrusted with cynicism.

By the beginning of the 1990s, it was becoming clear that no amount of empowering would create an orchestra if the members couldn't play their instruments. Empowerment was not discredited, but it was sidelined as a corporate mantra. Business thinking next took both trends (the organizational focus and the people-development focus) to new levels.

THE INCREASED SOPHISTICATION OF THE NINETIES

By the early 1990s, the debate was becoming more clearly defined, with a stronger emphasis on organizational leadership than on people leadership. The organizational focus took two tracks: the more technical track of systems thinking and the less tangible track of corporate culture.

Systems thinking was in part a response to the empowerment message of the 1980s, but it worked from an organizational perspective. The driver for organizational change, according to this thinking, comes not from empowering people directly but from changing the systems and structures that disempower them. It was this approach that propelled the rise of TQM (total quality management) and BPR (business process reengineering), the resurgence of Deming, and the prominence of academics such as Peter Senge (author of *The Fifth Discipline*). To counter the disappointment of empowerment and the ineffectiveness of empowering people who don't have the skills to use that empowerment, the focus turned to systems, driven in part by the assumption that redesigning the systems and structures would institutionalize and promote employee empowerment. With an empowered workforce in place (thanks to the right systems), it seemed all the organization needed was sophisticated, visionary leadership to be propelled to new levels of corporate performance. It didn't turn out to be that simple, but we still got the benefit of systems thinking.

Systems thinking—an essential concept for a leader to grasp— brought remarkable innovations and sophistication to work processes. The systems focus actually overlapped both organizational leadership and operational leadership (management): when systems were viewed organizationally as a whole, it was an alignment issue, thus an organizational leadership issue (BPR took this bigger perspective), and where it developed more of a task or operational focus (TQM for the most part), it took a management dimension and thus became more of an operational leadership issue.

The personality and character of the organization had their roots in corporate culture (whose roots were in anthropology), a notion that was studied and popularized by authors such as Edgar Schein (*Organizational Culture and Leadership*) and Terrence Deal and Allan Kennedy (*Corporate Cultures*). Several constructs emerged for measuring and evaluating corporate cultures (more on those later), and we began to see much closer attention paid to what people spoke of as the "soul" of the organization.

The field took a new boost with the publication of Jim Collins and Jerry Porras' *Built to Last,* a study of companies that had successfully maintained above-average performance levels over multiple generations. In each of the eighteen cases in the study (including household names like 3M, American Express, GE, IBM, Johnson & Johnson, Marriott, Sony, and Disney), a company was compared to another company in the same industry that at least at the outset had a similar profile, and the study tracked and compared the performance of each. In each case, it was the clear definition and articulation of a distinct set of values, as well as a compelling description of the company's future, that distinguished the visionary companies from the comparison companies.

The research was the first systematic study of the deeper drives and motivations of an organization. It was a compelling reinforcement for the power of a clear core ideology and a captivating and well-articulated future, anchored around an overarching goal big enough to capture the imagination and enlist the efforts of all within the organization. Its chief value lay in underscoring the impact of harnessing the intangibles of an organization to its direction.

THE REVIVED INTEREST IN THE LEADER'S PEOPLE-DEVELOPMENT ROLE

In the early 1990s, the field was dominated by the organizational focus just described. But in the second half of the decade, it became clear that neither visionary leadership nor empowerment nor systems thinking were directly addressing the people dimension of leadership—what leaders need to do to develop their people. Organizations were also beginning to recognize the vacuum left by the downsized middle management: people weren't being developed because fewer middle managers were around to develop them. Managers were increasingly reinstated, often renamed coaches, a concept that reflected the new interest in people leadership. For a while, coaching was also reinforced by the team-building movement, which gathered steam in the 1980s and became somewhat spent in the 1990s. Team building still remains important, but it has had a mixed record, mainly because team building is a methodology, not a principle; its status has been closely tied to empowerment, and it rose and fell with the fortunes of empowerment.

Coaching was also a popular concept because of its roots in sports. Business draws its analogies and inspiration primarily from three sources: sports, warfare, and biology (a distant third). The analogies are never complete: not many businesses can operate with the autocracy of a football team (nor, for that matter, with its salaries). And using the language doesn't necessarily make the difference; one of my clients at the time started calling supervisors "coaches" and employees "players," but whatever changes came did not come primarily because of a change in titles. Coaching nonetheless helped shape the debate; the late 1990s even saw the beginning and widespread acknowledgment of a new profession: corporate coaching.

Until the mid-1990s, research that validated the people dimension of leadership was relatively sparse. The University of Tel Aviv conducted some research on the impact of a soldier's relationship with his commanding officer in combat conditions, but it was relatively limited in scope. The greatest validation for the people dimension of leadership came from a Gallup research project (written up in *First, Break All the Rules*) that powerfully underscored the importance of a people focus in leadership.

The 1990s were also significant for another reason. With a go-go economy and a high demand for financially and operationally savvy leaders to capitalize on the opportunities of what was to become an overheated economy, character in leadership took a backseat to competence. How much you made was more important than how you made it, and the economic drop after the turn of the twenty-first century surfaced many of the ethical malpractices of corporate leaders. Once again, character entered into the debate over great leadership, bringing it greater depth—and more confusion.

TIME FOR INTEGRATION

The history of leadership has been the history of an evolution from the simple to the complex. Leadership in America grew up in an environment of homogeneous values, where leadership was mostly autocratic, often benevolent, and at times courageous and inspiring. It was also practiced within organizations of relatively manageable scope and scale. Over the course of the twentieth century, however, leadership evolved into a far more complex undertaking because the contexts in which leadership was exercised were themselves far more complex. The confusion generated by this complexity came to a head in the past twenty-five to thirty years, which have witnessed the groping attempts to provide alternatives to the dominance of the management and operational focus of the postwar decades. The alternatives focused on organizational leadership approaches on one hand and on people development solutions on the other. In the meantime, the previously dominant management and operational focus has been much maligned, but it hasn't gone away. Nor should it—any more than the other two should go away.

Instead, what we need is the integration of all three into a coherent whole. For leaders to lead well and for organizations to be well led, all three dimensions of leadership are necessary—organizational, operational, and people leadership. All three need to be integrated, and all three need to be fully and appropriately applied by those who should be applying them. A well-led organization (see Figure 3) is an organization in which all three find their fullest expression. Distinct but interdependent, each is critical to your organization's success— and equally critical to your personal success.

It's time to restore leadership to a manageable complexity. It's time to avoid oversimplification on one hand and obfuscation on the

FIGURE 3. THE THREE DIMENSIONS OF LEADERSHIP

other. It's time to provide a framework that clarifies the relationship each of the three dimensions has with the other two. It's time to give leaders, whatever their role, the blueprint for exercising great leadership in all its fullness.

Helping you apply these three dimensions of leadership—and helping you achieve the success that comes with it—is what this book is about. But, first, let's step back and look at the complete picture of leadership.

3

THE COMPLETE PICTURE ON LEADERSHIP

Understanding the Anatomy of Leadership

If anyone asked you to describe the essence of human nature, it's unlikely you'd start with an analysis of the human body. Despite its enormous complexity—just listen to a group of doctors arguing over a single diagnosis—we are not simply the sum of the chemical compounds that make up the visible and tangible expressions of who we are. What is visible and tangible—the way we behave, the way we look—is the expression of our aspirations, longings, and talents. It is what is within that defines us.

So it is with leadership. Much of leadership is invisible and intangible, and leadership behaviors are simply the expression of the invisible and intangible. In its most basic form, the anatomy of leadership is a matter of character and competence, as shown in Figure 4, where character has to do with the leader's inner drives and personal qualities and competence has to do with the leader's knowledge, skills, and talents. Character and competence combine to give us

FIGURE 4. ANATOMY OF LEADERSHIP: BASIC ELEMENTS

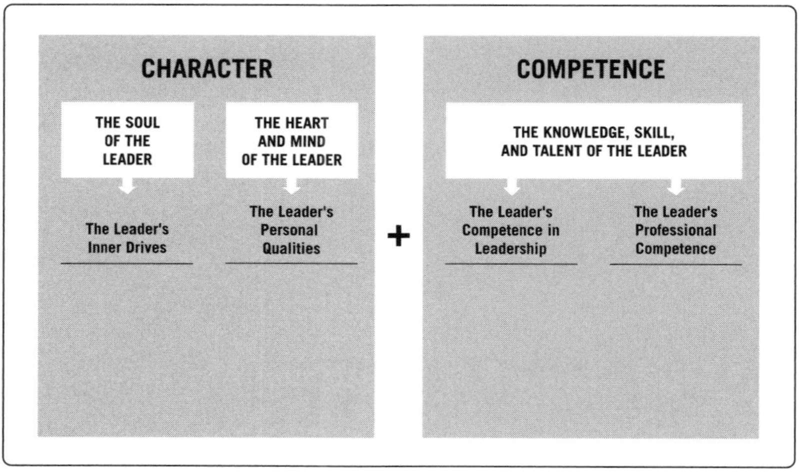

the heart, mind, soul, and talent of the leader—the anatomy of leadership.

These distinctions are far from academic, because every day leaders are being selected and groomed based on a narrow qualification for leadership (see Figure 5). In today's business climate, most leaders are selected because of their particular expertise and competence in a technical field—"professional competence" in Figure 4. That professional competence may have to do with expertise in a particular industry or market; it may be a functional expertise such as marketing, accounting, sales, engineering, or information technology; it may also be the business acumen to start a company or expand it. Whatever the professional competence, it is still only one element in the anatomy of leadership. The ultimate success of the selection will be the leader's capacity in the other elements—the leader's character as a leader and the leader's competence as a leader . . . both of which will be unpacked in the chapters that follow.

THE CHARACTER–COMPETENCE DEBATE

The nature of great leadership is an ancient debate. From the beginning of time, poor leadership has been endured and good leadership honored. In ancient Jewish history, King David was described as lead-

FIGURE 5. ANATOMY OF LEADERSHIP: CURRENT KEY TO SUCCESS

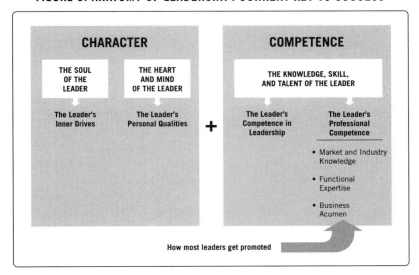

ing his people "with integrity of heart and skillfulness of hands"—poetic code for character and competence that set a standard few of his successors measured up to. But it wasn't until the birth of Greek civilization that the debate over the source and nature of great leadership began in earnest.

The Greeks gave the debate its impetus for two reasons. The first has to do with the gods of Greek mythology, who were essentially humans, flawed with all the whims and foibles of human nature but endowed with superhuman powers. Around these gods grew an impressive body of literature, describing heroes who were often not the gods themselves but those who defied them. The Greeks thus gave us an anecdotal study of great leadership.

The second reason has to do with the birth of democracy. As the Greeks initiated and established a form of government based on an open and accessible meritocracy, the debate on the essence of leadership moved from the realm of literary eloquence to the reality of practical governance. Because leadership was now much more broadly accessible, the question became What kind of leaders are we looking for? What defines great leadership?

The debate quickly turned on character and competence, and that debate was first argued in depth by Socrates. Socrates never actually wrote anything, but his discussions and thinking were captured by

Plato, Xenophon, and Aristotle, all three strong thinkers in their own right. For our purposes, the leadership debate was best captured by Xenophon, the least well-known of the three.

Socrates defined leadership in terms of competence. "Under all human conditions," he argued, "human beings are most willing to obey those whom they believe to be the best. Thus in sickness they most readily obey the doctor, on board ship the pilot, on the farm the farmer, whom they think to be most skilled in his business." It is much more likely, he argues, "that one who clearly knows best what ought to be done will most easily gain the obedience of the others." These comments, captured by Xenophon, clearly underscore the importance Socrates attached to competence in leadership.

Xenophon wasn't quite so sure. He argued that leaders can be highly competent, but if that is the only basis for their leadership, people will follow them not because they want to but because they must. For people to want to follow a leader, the leader needs qualities of character, not just competence. Xenophon identified thirteen key qualities of great leadership:

Temperance	Sympathy
Justice	Helpfulness
Sagacity	Courage
Amiability	Magnanimity
Presence of mind	Generosity
Tactfulness	Considerateness
Humanity	

Aristotle was much less complicated. He identified four leadership qualities: justice, temperance, prudence, and fortitude.

Thus began a debate that has never subsided. Ever since the days of Socrates, Aristotle, and Xenophon, character and competence have lived in tension. But that debate has arguably never been as intense as it is now. In the 1990s, all the emphasis was on competence with little thought to character, leading to the many spectacular scandals in recent years, where issues of character derailed otherwise highly competent leaders. But leaders can also fail for lack of competence, especially in our complex world where the exercise of leadership is more demanding than it's ever been. Ultimately, leaders fail either because they don't understand the mechanics of leadership in all its complexity (competence) or because they break trust with those they lead and the community they serve (character).

If competence gets you to the table, it's character that keeps you there. As Stanford University's Jeffrey Pfeffer has pointed out, the reason we have seen so much corruption surface in recent years may be that the business schools these highly competent and gifted leaders went to gave them the technical tools without the moral compass to use them. They got to the table because they used the tools well, but they were then dismissed when they failed to use them appropriately.

Os Guinness, an observer and commentator on American society for the past thirty years, argues, "One of the central and most important issues in Western civilization [is] the relationship between character and the free person, the good life, the just community, and the strong, wise leader." Political scientist James Q. Wilson observes that there is a "growing awareness that a variety of public problems can only be understood—and perhaps addressed—if they are seen as arising out of a defect in character formation." Guinness applies this directly to leadership: "Far from a cliché or a matter of hollow civic piety, character in leaders is important for two key reasons: Externally, character provides the point of trust that links leaders with followers; internally, character is the part-gyroscope, part-brake that provides the leader's strongest source of bearings and restraint. In many instances the first prompting to do good and the last barrier against doing wrong are the same—character."

The essence of great leadership—and the solution to the tension between character and competence—is giving due importance to both.

RESOLVING THE TENSION

Great leaders, then, are great because they are both competent and noble. Great leadership requires both; you cannot have one without the other. Some leaders demonstrate neither, some demonstrate one but not the other, and a few (rare but real) demonstrate both. The practice of leadership is very different in each case, and the grid in Figure 6 on the following page, which was developed with one of my colleagues, Dan Shoultz, addresses the tension between the two.

In the bottom left quadrant (low character and low competence), we find leaders who are both inept and untrustworthy. It may be tempting to dismiss such leaders as roadkill, but it turns out that more leaders camp in this quadrant than anyone would like to admit.

FIGURE 6. CHARACTER-COMPETENCE GRID

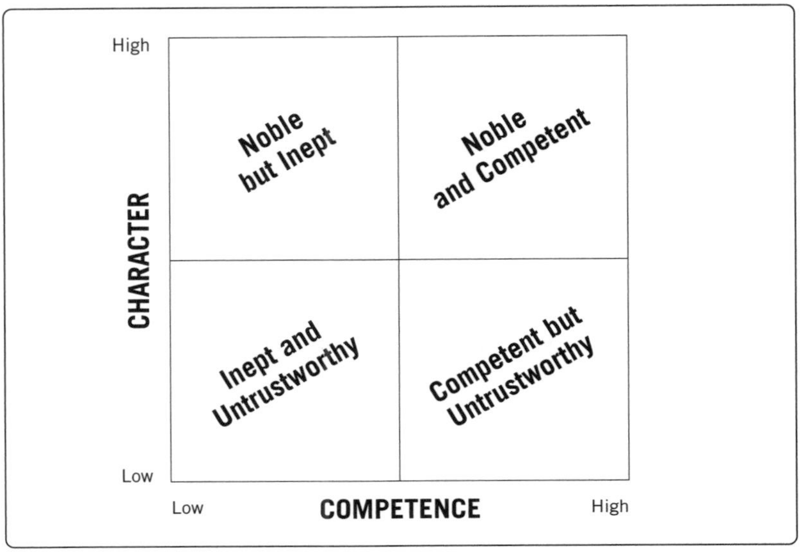

Barbara Kellerman at Harvard's Center for Public Leadership has developed a typology of bad leadership, motivated at least in part by the amazing capacity people have for tolerating corrupt, stupid, mean, and self-serving leadership. We may not live in a totalitarian state, but our society has plenty of pockets where totalitarian leadership is freely exercised.

The top right quadrant (high character and high competence) is clearly the ideal, where leadership is both noble and competent. This is a rarified atmosphere, and not many leaders have the stamina to keep climbing to get there. It is far from inaccessible, however, nor is it reserved only for those who are uniquely wired. No leader is born into that quadrant. Leaders get there by the lessons they learn and the choices they make.

The other two are the thornier quadrants. Leaders with high competence and low character (the bottom right quadrant) are essentially competent but untrustworthy, even corrupt. They are gifted but dangerous. We typically respect their competence and we may even admire them, but we don't let our guard down. We tend to live with them and tolerate them: the gifted but corrupt leader at least gets results, and, if we like the results, we overlook the manner in which they were obtained.

Leaders with high character and low competence (the top left quadrant) are noble but inept—they have high standards and high ideals, but they lack the competence to implement them. These are almost harder to work with than those in the bottom right quadrant; because we like and respect them, we don't want to see them fail, and their strong character makes their ineptitude all the more painful to experience. When a corrupt leader is brought down, we feel a sense of justice; not so when noble leaders fall because of incompetence. We are more likely to feel sorrow or disappointment.

Think of leaders you have worked for—which quadrant best describes them? Think of past and recent political leaders—which quadrant would you put them in? Where would you put Jefferson, Adams, and Washington? What about Lincoln, FDR, Truman, and Martin Luther King Jr.? Where would you put Hitler and Stalin? Saddam Hussein? Jimmy Carter, Ronald Reagan, George H. W. Bush, Bill Clinton, and George W. Bush? Margaret Thatcher and Tony Blair? What about business leaders like Henry Ford, Tom Watson, Sam Walton, Lee Iacocca, Dennis Kozlowski, and Martha Stewart?

Where, most important of all, would you put yourself?

Before pursuing the intriguing task of assigning different leaders to different quadrants (and the more uncomfortable task of choosing a quadrant as a personal space), however, it's best to stop and bring some definition to *character* and *competence*.

What Is Character?

Character is not personality; it is not primarily defined by the preferences and makeup a person is born with, though it is most certainly influenced by them. Character is fundamentally about choices: character determines how competence will be used and to what ends it will be applied. Competence can be used for good or evil, and character determines that choice. This is what Larry Bossidy calls "moral fortitude."

Character is not just about ends; it's also about means. It's one thing to pursue noble ends and quite another to pursue them with noble means. Both are the essence of character, which gives the following definition:

Character in leadership is pursuing noble ends with noble means.

Character in leadership is absent when either aspect is absent (noble ends or noble means). It's not enough to have noble ends; how you pursue them is just as important. Noble ends without noble means is leadership without character.

What constitutes a noble end? How do we know if the purpose we are pursuing is inherently worthy? We can acknowledge ends as worthy if

- They are other-focused

- They are not self-aggrandizing

- They contribute and add value

- They are larger than self

Ends are other-focused when they are unselfish, when they are concerned with the good of others both inside and outside the organization. They are not self-aggrandizing when they avoid being driven by personal ambition and individual empire building. They contribute and add value when they improve or enhance the lives of those they serve. This covers a great deal, from food services to clothing to housing to recreation—each serves a noble, legitimate, and worthy cause. It's actually easier to identify what doesn't qualify, and the list is fairly obvious—drug trafficking, prostitution, and so on—anything that ends up destroying either those who use it or those who deliver it.

A noble end is larger than its holder's immediate context—it will be larger than an individual, a unit, an organization; it places the holder's daily routine in the context of a broader contribution. Churchill was not just fighting Hitler; he was fighting for the Empire and for freedom from tyranny. In World War I, after he was fired as First Lord of the Admiralty, he took a command on the western front, and, as his granddaughter Celia Sandys puts it, "he reveled at being a small part of a noble cause." When Sony was launched in the aftermath of World War II, its ambition was to change the perception of Japanese products and Japanese culture—an end far greater than the scope of its business. The National Institute for Learning Disabilities aims to transform the way people think about the learning disabled—an end far greater than the scope of the organization.

Many leaders have pursued ends that were undeniably noble, but they compromised their leadership by applying means that were anything but noble. Noble means are those where the ends are pursued with personal qualities such as these:

- Integrity

- Focus

- Courage

- Care for others

- Humility

Integrity suggests honesty, fairness, justice, and dependability. An end pursued with dishonest, unfair, or unjust means destroys the trust people give their leaders. Great leaders recognize that the ends never justify the means, whatever the personal cost.

Focus is about purpose and direction. Great leaders have a point on the horizon that provides the focus of their attention; their eyes rarely stray from it, they see it clearly, and they describe it well.

Focus requires the courage to confront conflict, to risk life, to risk reputation, to learn from mistakes, and to keep persevering. The higher the stakes in terms of the ends, the greater the courage needed in the pursuit of those ends. The founding fathers put much more at risk than we do in our daily professional existence, and few of us are likely to be called on to demonstrate the kind of courage they did. Nonetheless, when our integrity is challenged, doing what is right requires the courage to confront conflict and risk the loss of a reputation and, in some cases, a job. At the very least, we constantly confront the challenge of learning from our mistakes and taking honest ownership of them. For Churchill, courage was the greatest of all leadership qualities; he amply demonstrated it, both physically and morally.

Focus also calls for a commitment consuming enough that we are willing to make sacrifices for it. This is what Jim Collins calls the "tremendous ambition for the cause, the company, the work—but not for themselves—and the unbelievably terrifying will to make good on that." This "unbelievably terrifying will" is the consuming commitment and willingness to make sacrifices that others may not be willing to make. John Adams endured long separations from his wife, Abigail, at one time for five straight years; he bore the brunt of slander and misunderstanding; he sacrificed financially; and he expended tremendous energy and effort to win others over to the cause of independence, all the while agonizing over the birth of the new republic. His reputation in England was such that he was singled out for hanging without consideration for pardon in the event that the fight for independence was lost.

Without a genuine care for the people in our charge and for the beneficiaries of the service they provide, leaders' focus and courage are self-serving. Great generals, great business leaders, and great statesmen have not necessarily been nice to the people they led (at times, quite the contrary), but they did care about what mattered to them. The loyalty of Napoleon's soldiers was earned mostly because he cared about their condition and survival; that loyalty even survived his foolish and ill-advised invasion of Russia.

Integrity, focus, and courage without care and humility make for arrogantly self-righteous leaders. Humility is the ingredient that keeps leaders approachable, that allows them to laugh at themselves, that keeps them from taking themselves too seriously, and that keeps them learning and growing. Collins found this ingredient (along with the "tremendous ambition for the cause") in the leaders who led their companies out of the middle of the pack to outstrip all the rest.

By these measures, some of the icons of history begin to lose their sheen. Jefferson, for example, was extraordinarily competent and gifted, and his contribution to the cause of independence was immense. But his reputation as a great leader was marred by the some of the means he chose in the pursuit of his ends. He opposed slavery but maintained slaves to support his lifestyle (not to mention a slave he kept as a mistress). He took up noble political causes but paid journalists to smear his political opponents. He stands in strong contrast to Washington and Adams, whose ends were the same as Jefferson's, but who, unlike Jefferson, pursued the same ends with undeniable integrity, courage, sacrifice, and humility.

What made Adams different from Jefferson? The difference was much more profound than a simple difference in their behavior as leaders. It had to do with their inner drives—their inner world as leaders. For us as for them, that inner world is shaped by three key drives: our philosophy of leadership, our moral compass, and our level of self-awareness—as outlined in Figure 7. Every leader has a philosophy of leadership, but, for most, it is underdeveloped and largely unreasoned. Every great leader has a moral compass, and, at some point, every great leader draws a line in the sand and stakes a position on that line. And every great leader has huge doses of self-awareness; great leaders know not only their aspirations but also their strengths and weaknesses.

FIGURE 7. ANATOMY OF LEADERSHIP: ELEMENTS OF CHARACTER

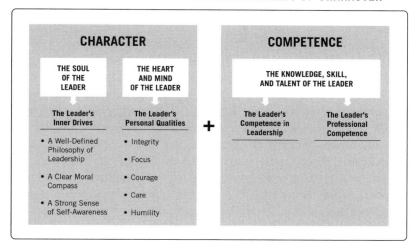

The deeper inner drives of a leader at least in part explain why some leaders can pursue an ignoble end with at least some noble means. Al Capone had no fear of conflict and at times exhibited great courage. Even Hitler was no doubt loyal to his henchmen. But good means don't justify poor ends. There is honor among thieves, but that doesn't make thievery honorable. The choice of ends is made in the leader's inner world, in obedience to the inner compass the leader decides to follow.

What Is Competence?

For leaders to be genuinely competent, they need to demonstrate

- Professional competence

- Leadership competence

As noted earlier, a leader's professional competence might rest on a particular industry or market expertise. Because of the actual or per-ceived complexity of a particular sector, a history and experience in that sector is often heavily weighted in a selection decision. The business challenges, financial structures, and marketing imperatives of a hospital, a Chamber of Commerce, a nonprofit philanthropic organization, a consumer products manufacturer, a financial services company, a government contractor, a consulting company, and a mass-market service company are all very different, and professional competence requires some measure of comfort within a particular sector. Fresh blood can be good, but the learning curve may be too arduous to meet the expectations thrust on the leader in the time frame that most new leaders are given.

A leader's professional competence might also be based on a particular functional expertise such as engineering, marketing, sales, or finance. In today's increasingly complex regulatory environment, the profile of financial expertise has been significantly raised, and more chief financial officers are moving into the chief executive's office. A leader's professional competence might also come from the business acumen to start a company or expand it, whether through natural growth or acquisition.

Professional competence is overrated in leadership. Important though it is, it isn't indispensable to great leadership. Leadership competence, however, is. You can survive as a leader with weak professional competence if your leadership competence is strong; it will be much harder to live out a lifetime of great leadership if your leadership competence is weak, however strong your professional competence.

Professional competence is what business schools teach: the financial and operational mechanisms of an organization and the tools for the quantitative measurement of business performance. Students become mathematically and statistically grounded, and they learn the science of business. But they are not introduced to the art of leadership.

Leadership competence means understanding how different levels of leadership responsibility require different kinds of leadership approach, applied appropriately to the right level. Leadership as a CEO is exercised differently from leadership of a business unit or leadership of a production team in a manufacturing plant. Organizations need to be led, tasks need to be led, and people need to be led, and in each case the leadership skills are different. Few leaders make the distinction between these different expressions of leadership, and without making distinctions, leadership competence is compromised —and so is leadership effectiveness.

Organizations are complex organisms, and leadership competence requires understanding how they work and how to change them. A deficiency here may well be behind the striking increase in senior

FIGURE 8. ANATOMY OF LEADERSHIP: THE FULL STORY

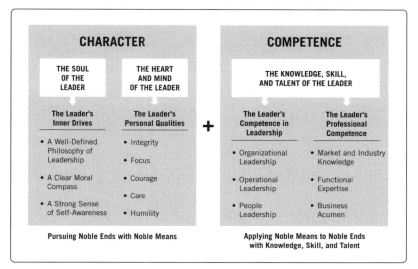

executive turnover, a disturbing feature of today's business climate. New CEOs, division leaders, or department heads are often greeted with high expectations; they engage in sweeping reform, mostly counterproductive and unsuccessful, and when the reforms fail, they are dumped unceremoniously. The real issue is that few leaders truly understand what it takes to transform an organization. They don't have the leadership competence that would give them the organizational insight they need.

Competence is a matter of degree, and the degrees are best described in terms of knowledge, skill, and talent (see Figure 8). Some leaders have an innate ability, a talent, to exercise these competences, and others exercise them because they underwent the discipline of acquiring the necessary knowledge and practicing the appropriate skills. But even in the case of a leader with a high level of talent, that competence still needs to be learned and practiced. Michael Jordan would never have been as great a basketball player as he was, for all his talent, if he hadn't been extraordinarily disciplined in developing it.

These distinctions add up to the following definition:

Competence in leadership is applying noble means to noble ends with knowledge, skill, and talent.

FIGURE 9. CHARACTER-COMPETENCE INTERPLAY

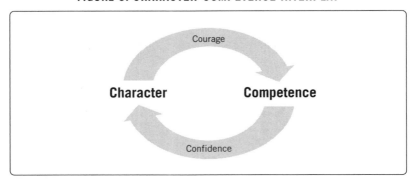

The Interplay between Character and Competence

In great leaders, character and competence are symbiotic. Character breeds courage, and courage strengthens competence; competence breeds confidence, and confidence strengthens character (see Figure 9). Churchill's granddaughter Celia Sandys observed that Churchill "understood war from top to bottom—as a journalist, a field commander, and an administrator. He knew how armies worked, and knew the factors that helped them win." That competence bred hisconfidence—as Sandys put it, that "knowledge fed his innate optimism." That confidence in turn strengthened his courage to stick to noble means in the pursuit of his noble ends.

Character also feeds competence. Churchill knew about flying because he learned to fly; he understood its strategic importance— which is why he learned to fly. It was an act of considerable courage, and that courage bred competence. He understood better than any of his contemporaries the potential impact of air power on warfare, and it became part of his strategy. The character he demonstrated in understanding the nature of flying considerably enhanced his competence as a leader.

THE CHALLENGE OF MAINTAINING THE TENSION

Maintaining the balance between character and competence—ascribing due importance to both—is notoriously difficult. Leaders who embody both are rare indeed.

Typically, character gets short-changed. The primary measure in recruitment today is competence, with only scant attention paid to character. That's in part because it's no small challenge to assess the character of someone you barely know. But even more intense is the pressure for results that compel organizations to look for people who above all else deliver those results, so they turn a blind eye to the character issues that surface in the pursuit of those results. At some point, however, the short-term gains of competence at the expense of character become slight in comparison to the long-term losses incurred by the absence of character. That's when an organization loses its soul; and, when it loses its soul, it loses its credibility. When it loses its credibility, it loses its leaders. When it loses its leaders, it loses its destiny.

It is character and not competence that lingers with us long after a leader is gone. But character doesn't just have to do with warm memories; character in leadership also has an undeniably very present impact on an organization. Rob Lebow's remarkable study of 17 million surveys identified eight key concepts that explained high-performing organizations, eight concepts embraced and lived out by their leaders: treating others with uncompromising truth, trusting people, mentoring unselfishly, being receptive to new ideas whatever their origin, taking risks for the organization, giving credit where credit is due, being honest, and putting the interests of others first. Yes, it's the stuff you learned in grade school. But character is powerful.

And yet without competence, leaders with impeccable character cannot be great. And that is the essence of leadership: ascribing due importance to both character and competence, emphasizing both, short-changing neither.

Thinking back to Figure 6, on page 38, what quadrant are you in? It's not a rhetorical question: how you answer will determine how you shape your leadership curriculum. If you want to delve further into the issues of character, read straight on to Part II. If you want to focus on leadership competence, jump to Part III. But whichever you go to first, don't neglect the other; you need both to exercise great leadership.

Whichever you choose to focus on first, the purpose of this book is to help you climb into the top right quadrant, staking your ground among the noble and the competent. The climb is hard, but the view is worth it.

PART II

CHARACTER IN LEADERSHIP

Soul, Heart, and Mind

4

THE SOUL OF
THE LEADER

Looking at Your Leadership Style—from the Inside Out

A senior vice president at one of my client companies once strode into a meeting, and—somewhere between the door and his chair—announced that his right leg was sore from kicking everyone in the rear end all day (in stronger and more colorful language). The tone of the meeting was set, but, more significantly, the philosophy behind his leadership style was exposed—a personal philosophy of people, contribution, motivation, and leadership that shaped the way he behaved as a leader (and, just to be clear, one you don't want to emulate).

If his actions betray a philosophy of leadership, is the same true for everyone? You bet it is. Do you have a personal philosophy of leadership? You bet you do. And it shapes the way you lead—far more than you realize. Just like this VP, all leaders have reactions and behaviors that are shaped, consciously or unconsciously, by their philosophy of leadership.

For most leaders—just like this VP—those behaviors are shaped unconsciously, because most leaders give little or no thought to

FIGURE 10. WHAT DRIVES LEADERS' BEHAVIORS: THE BASICS

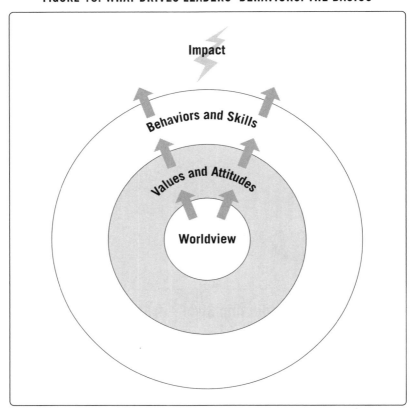

the philosophy that drives their behaviors. The whole training and development industry—an $80 billion industry by some estimates—doesn't help, because training and development tends to focus on visible behaviors rather than on the unconscious philosophy that drives them. Leadership is much more than acquiring the right set of behaviors. Although behaviors inevitably need to be addressed, such a focus follows an outside-in approach, treating symptoms rather than causes. Instead, leaders need an inside-out approach: developing a sound philosophy from which sound behaviors can flow.

Figure 10 highlights the real drivers behind leadership behaviors. Leadership behaviors and skills—what you actually do as a leader and the skills you possess, represented by the outer circle—are actually driven by values (the next circle in), which in turn are shaped by your worldview (the very center circle).

Most of the time, effort, and money spent on leadership training and development is focused on the outer circle (behaviors and skills), mainly because behavioral or skill-based problems are the easiest to detect, discuss, and correct. This focus is driven by the assumption that behaviors can be taught and absorbed on their own merit, which is only partially true. While some skills and behaviors can improve with training and awareness, their long-term assimilation into behavior will be determined far more by the level of thought given to the value of those behaviors. You don't plant a cactus in a rain forest; it won't take root in a hostile soil. Unless the behaviors you are teaching are planted in a receptive worldview, they won't take root.

A philosophy of leadership is the common denominator in all great leaders. They think about it, and they are very intentional in the way they think about it. They translate experience, observation, and reading into a philosophy of leadership that governs their practice of leadership. Their worldview guides and informs them, and they operate from a set of principles and values that drive and shape their behaviors as leaders.

Worldview and values, however, are nebulous concepts, especially in a business climate that deals with concrete substance, cutthroat negotiations, pressing deadlines, and sleep-destroying unpredictability. If, however, we disregard the underlying worldview and values that drive our leadership behaviors, not only will great leadership be compromised, but we will also be more prone to the kind of leadership behaviors that have led to the now-commonplace downfalls and bankruptcies of the past few years. Building your leadership on a sound philosophy is the best antidote to such a fate; it will transform your leadership style—not from the outside in but from the inside out.

So how leaders think determines how they lead. To lead well, think well.

THE PARADIGM TRAP

To think well, we must challenge our existing assumptions—what scientists and psychologists call our paradigms. That's easier said than done. An experience in Brazil reminded me just how tenacious my own paradigms can be. Four of us were making a four-hour car trip from Rio de Janeiro to a coastal town called Paraty, 150 miles south of Rio (for four non-Portuguese-speaking gringos, a foolish rather than gutsy undertaking). After several hours of driving and several abortive attempts to get directions, we eventually found someone who could accurately pinpoint us on the map.

We were expecting to be near our destination; the reality was much worse. After two hours of driving, we had turned onto the right road—but in the wrong direction. When we thought we were going south, we were in reality going north. We were now actually farther away from our destination than our original starting point.

We missed the clues. We drove past a large mansion half-hidden by trees. "Hey," one of us said, "Haven't we seen something like that before?" We had seen the very same building driving into Rio two days earlier. "Popular architecture," we concluded. Rio has a big bay with a long bridge, and, as we were crossing this bridge, mistaking the view for a city further south, we saw the open sea to our right, not on our left as it should have been. Instead of concluding we were going north, we assumed that the bay was very big.

With the right paradigm, we would have recognized some of Rio's characteristic landmarks despite the distance, but we were locked into a southbound paradigm, a filter that distorted reality. When we later embraced the right paradigm, our earlier conclusions appeared foolish (that would have to be one enormous bay), but at the time they seemed reasonable. More accurately, they were *preferable:* we didn't want to entertain a northbound paradigm. Most disturbing was that we were looking at scenes we would probably have recognized if we had been in the right paradigm.

It is small comfort knowing that such tenacious commitment to misplaced paradigms is all too common. The business climate can at times be as unfamiliar as Brazil was to my companions and me, so it's common to see businesses not recognizing market changes, employees not embracing new organizational realities, leaders not responding to changing needs in the workforce and instead clinging to misaligned management styles—all examples of where paradigms shift and their holders don't.

To lead well, you must think well, and to think well, you must challenge your own thinking patterns. The good patterns will withstand the scrutiny; the poor ones shouldn't. And, in the process, you will clarify your worldview.

YOUR WORLDVIEW

If you want to be a great leader, there's no avoiding this look inside, and there's no avoiding the learning and probing that comes with it. But it's well worth the effort; you will join the ranks of those great men and women, known and unknown, who have been driven and guided by a well-defined worldview and a well-articulated set of core values.

Not all worldviews, however, are created equal, and not just any worldview will do—unless you are willing to lump Hitler, Stalin, Al Capone, and Jim Jones in with George Washington, John Adams, Abraham Lincoln, and Winston Churchill. Every one of these leaders had a well-defined worldview and well-articulated values, but there is no equality between the worldview of a Hitler and that of a Lincoln—where one sought to eliminate the marginal and the other to free them.

So what do I mean by worldview? And what makes for a good worldview? Defining a personal worldview means figuring out what life is about and how we fit into it. It's how we look at the world and how we interpret what goes on in it. We all have a worldview, a way of explaining and understanding everything that happens during the course of the day, and, however undefined and unclear, that worldview is in there somewhere, gestating and looking for expression. At its most basic level, our worldview explains to our own satisfaction the universe and its origin, the existence or nonexistence of God, the nature of humankind, the means of contribution, and the nature of destiny. For some, the answers are clear; for others, the questions are still unanswered.

Wherever you are in your quest for answers, you can define your philosophy of leadership by addressing three key concepts:

- The source of your authority as a leader

- Your view of human nature

- Your sense of purpose and destiny

The Source of Your Authority as a Leader

Leadership is an issue of authority, and we all frame the source of our authority in one of two ways: internally or externally. If we frame it internally, we ourselves define the measure of right or wrong;

we decide what is good or bad. We also allow everyone else to frame their own source internally, however much we may disagree with the way they frame it. If we ascribe authority externally, we acknowledge some outside standard or source of right and wrong, good and bad, and measure our performance, and that of others, by that external standard.

The dividing line is the concept of absolutes. If we acknowledge absolutes, we implicitly acknowledge an external standard; if we don't acknowledge absolutes, we implicitly define right and wrong by an internal standard and we also acknowledge everyone else's right to define right and wrong by their own internal standard. This makes it difficult to condemn someone else's standard; if someone's internal standard allows for rape and theft, for example, we cannot censure them—why should one person's standard necessarily be better than someone else's? If you rebel against this argument, you believe implicitly in absolutes.

I'm hard-pressed to think of a single great leader who didn't buy into the notion of absolutes in some form or other. Many great leaders believed in some absolute they not only were willing to die for but also were willing to recruit others to die for. At some point, every great leader says, "That's enough." They don't all draw their line in the same place and they don't all define absolutes the same way— for instance, some of Churchill's and Gandhi's were diametrically opposed.

Defining right and wrong is a hot topic in corporate practice today. Seeing senior executives being led away in handcuffs on prime-time TV gives pause to any business leader and should push each of us to think about those boundaries we will not cross in compromising integrity. As a leader in the marketplace, defining your standard of right and wrong and the source of that standard is every bit as important as the quality of your product or service and the reputation it garners; in fact, defining that standard will determine more than anything else the quality and reputation of your products or services.

As leaders, we need our own personal creed of conduct, and that personal creed of conduct needs to be solidly founded on absolutes we believe in. The bottom line for you as a leader is How do you define right and wrong? And what do you base it on? That's where great leadership starts. Dennis Kozlowski, the fallen giant of Tyco, failed because he kept adjusting his definition of right and wrong. Small, inconsequential lies about his childhood and credentials gave way to substantial and very consequential lies to his board and investors. Competence projected him to fame; character—a lack of clarity about right and wrong and a lack of accountability—brought him infamy.

At one point during an engagement with a multibillion-dollar company, my colleagues and I were helping the business units align their regional strategies to the corporate strategy. During an executive team meeting at one of these business units—a $150 million enterprise in its own right—the finance director, with some courage, voiced the concern that the corporate office was asking him to take some actions he felt profoundly uncomfortable taking. The response from one of his senior colleagues was simply, "You must do what you think is best." That response was an invitation to follow his own standard of right and wrong, when in fact the finance director was looking to the senior leadership to define correct and incorrect action. Their response betrayed an abdication of their responsibility as leaders to define the values of the organization. We called them on it. Such an unwillingness to define right and wrong behavior creates a climate where a blind eye is turned to pushing the ethical envelope, and, left long enough, ends up in an Enron-style meltdown.

Your View of Human Nature

How you view human nature has many implications for how you lead. It will shape how you select people, how you motivate and develop them, and how you handle their mistakes. This is no new concept: more than forty years ago, Douglas McGregor contrasted two leadership styles based on different views of human nature—one where people are naturally lazy and resistant to work (what he called Theory X) and the other where people, given the right circumstances, are willing and eager to contribute their best (what he called Theory Y). That VP with the sore right leg has clearly bought into Theory X: he sees human beings as capable of productivity only with the use of a well-placed right foot.

The easiest way of defining human nature is to think of people as being both unique and fallible. Everyone is uniquely gifted and everyone is prone to mistakes. Since your view of people can have a dramatic impact on both your personal and professional relationships, grasping these two concepts is the cornerstone of effective leadership.

Intuitively, these two concepts make sense, but much of leadership practice actually contradicts them. If you buy into the notion that people can do pretty much anything they put their minds to—good as that may sound—you don't buy into the uniqueness of human nature. You will view differences of performance as simply differences of unfulfilled potential, and your focus will be on providing training to meet the deficiency. If you believe that people are absolutely unique, with unique gifts and talents, you will focus much more on matching their talents with the environment that allows those talents to blossom. Training and development will concentrate on improving their strengths. It will also change your selection criteria, because you will select to match talent to need, rather than assume you can train to match the need.

People are also fallible. If you have a low tolerance for human error, you probably don't subscribe to human fallibility. The more you believe in the perfectibility of human nature, the less tolerant you are of mistakes. There is plenty of evidence for the fallibility of human nature, but it is not politically correct to discuss it as such; we prefer to talk about "development needs" rather than "weaknesses." But the reality is that we all have weaknesses, and the smartest approach is to operate in an environment where our weaknesses don't count—and our strengths do.

Your Sense of Purpose and Destiny

Great leaders look at the world through the lens of a well-defined purpose. They believe they have a contribution to make. That purpose doesn't have to be on the grandiose level of preserving freedom and fighting tyranny, but it is nonetheless present at whatever level they exercise great leadership.

Of the three dimensions of worldview, this is the one that has been most easily embraced. Stephen Covey and others have done much to validate the impact of a well-crafted personal mission statement. Leaders who have embraced the notion and made the effort to draw up their own mission statement stand out for their quiet confidence, built on the assurance of a purpose that transcends the call of the bottom line. It provides intrinsic motivation to succeed by helping them understand a clear direction for their lives and align their decisions and behaviors to that direction.

This presupposes a willingness to reflect on paper—a willingness to write. It has been said that leaders are readers; true, and leaders are also writers. They may not be great writers; they may not spell well or use correct grammar; but they do write, using their fingers to exercise their brains. A few were great writers as well as great leaders, but most leaders aren't and don't need to be. They don't write for public consumption; they write in journals to clarify their thoughts. Writing helps them think, and thinking helps them lead.

With the incredibly tight schedule most leaders keep, the process of defining a personal mission may seem daunting. This, however, is at the core of your worldview. Your values and behaviors are shaped by your purpose. What is your passion in life? What are your strengths, gifts, greatest attributes? What do you want to leave as your legacy? How do you want to be viewed by others? What is your reason for being? Finding an answer to these questions can bring clarity to your worldview.

Your Values

Our values are shaped by our worldview. If our worldview reflects our core beliefs around the deeper questions of life, our values are the principles through which we express those core beliefs. If the glasses we put on every morning tell us that life is "solitary, nasty, brutish and short" (in the words of philosopher Thomas Hobbes), the values we consciously or unconsciously express throughout the day are likely to be correspondingly mercenary, protective, suspicious, and selfish. With less dark and gloomy glasses, our values will most likely be more expansive.

Values have the quality of deep-rooted conviction. They are held dearly and are entirely consistent with your worldview, even if subconsciously so; in fact, uncovering your values can help you understand your worldview. Values are typically few but firm. They are nonnegotiable. And, of course, they drive behavior.

Some personal values have a universal quality to them, and could just as easily be described as public virtues. The most obvious include integrity, equity, justice, commitment, trustworthiness, fidelity, loyalty, humility, industriousness, respect, consideration, kindness, patience, forgiveness, and generosity. Such universal virtues have a clear moral dimension; few argue against them, even if they don't live by them.

Great leadership reflects at least some of these virtues; people follow leaders who keep their word, who show respect, and who act with humility. And the extent to which leaders do so is a function of their sense of absolutes and their definition of right and wrong. Virtually all great leaders have integrated some of these virtues into their lives, and these virtues are never more evident than when tested. Jefferson attributed much of the success of the American Revolution to Washington's character: "The moderation and virtue of a single character probably prevented this Revolution from being closed, as most others have been, by a subversion of that liberty it was intended to establish." Many less prominent than Washington have exhibited the same strength of character—Dietrich Bonhoeffer, for example, the German pastor who returned to Germany from America before World War II and was hanged just weeks before the end of the war for his part in the resistance to Hitler. Bonhoeffer returned to Germany because, as he told a friend, "If I stayed [in America], I'd become a living lie to everything I believe in." His decisions were shaped by the deep inner convictions he held on right and wrong.

Other values are more individual. People typically hold these the closest and voice them the most promptly. They may be widespread, but they are not universal. Education, for example, is a value for many, but not for everyone, and not holding such a value carries no moral condemnation. For others, it might be the importance of family, or the value of work, or the pursuit of financial security. In antebellum America, it was land; land was the currency of success, and land was the real hero in *Gone with the Wind*. These values have no moral dimension, but those who hold them live by them. Great leaders know their own individual values, and articulate them well to the people they lead.

Real values are lived out with conviction. They define boundaries: they prescribe what we will do and won't do. The ultimate measure of a value is the price we are willing to pay to live by it. If someone claims family as a value but is having an affair, something else is more important than family, whatever that person may claim. Those who make sacrificial career choices for the good of their family can genuinely claim family as a value. Whatever your values, if you can't point to sacrifices you have made to live by them, question the sincerity of those values. The stronger your values, the easier those tough choices become; as Stephen Covey has pointed out, it's easier to say no when you have a higher yes.

Character in leadership is expressed mainly through the public virtues. The battle for character is won or lost in the leader's commitment to the public virtues, and if we think of great leaders of the past, those who stand out are the leaders whose lives were consistent with the public virtues they embraced. We remember them not only because they were gifted leaders but also because they were noble leaders.

This doesn't mean that you have to have this moral framework to get results, and plenty of leaders get spectacular results without such a framework. We don't remember them in the same way, and they often pay a high moral price to achieve their results. They are remembered, even admired, but their memory is seldom honored. In today's business climate of intensified scrutiny, the life span of a leader without a moral framework is shortening. The bullets are getting harder to dodge.

If this sounds too demanding a standard for leadership, take heart from the fact that this is what people are looking for in a leader. There's a deep hunger today for noble leadership that pursues noble ends with noble means. This hunger explains why "servant leadership" has come to be recognized as such a powerful form of leadership—it embodies the essentials of public virtues. Such leadership seeks primarily the good of the organization, the good of the people in it, and the good of those touched by it. It stakes out the moral high ground, and, interestingly, research bears out the remarkable impact and power of such leadership, whether it's the leadership described in Jim Collins's *Good to Great* or the leadership uncovered in Gallup's *First, Break All the Rules*. Collins saw a correlation between such leadership and the teachings of the great religions. "Without looking for it," he commented in an interview with John Maxwell, "we found a tremendous correlation between the types of leaders that took companies from good to great—using a clinical definition of results—and the teachings of the great religions. I don't even have a religious background. I certainly wasn't looking for this. But the data bore it out."

Strong, clearly articulated values are far more powerful than charisma in effective leadership. Great leaders gather followers because of their values and because of the consistency with which they apply them. This may in fact be the single most liberating concept in leadership: you don't have to be charismatic to be a great leader; you simply need to have a clear set of values, articulate them often, and live by them.

Self-Awareness

Great leaders have abundant self-awareness. Some consider this the defining characteristic of great leadership, because leaders who are aware of their limitations are more likely, on one hand, to recruit staff who compensate for their weaknesses and, on the other, to focus their energies around their own strengths.

Self-awareness also breeds authenticity, an endearing quality in leadership. Authenticity has to do with honesty; it's the willingness to tell the truth without sugarcoating it. It's an endearing quality because it tells people that they can be trusted by their leaders to handle the truth. But it's more than just being truthful about our circumstances; it's also about being truthful about ourselves. James Kouzes and Barry Posner's *Leadership Challenge* is just one of many reports of surveys that put honesty at the top of the qualities people are looking for in their leaders.

Authenticity also has to do with integrity: the assurance that what you are is what people see, so they know that what they see is what they get. Its antithesis is hypocrisy, and there is little people like less in a leader than the claim to be one thing while in reality being another—even if living the truth would mean admitting a reality they don't like. People prefer to deal with a wolf than with a wolf disguised as a sheep. Self-awareness doesn't guarantee authenticity, but authenticity is virtually impossible without it.

Such self-awareness encompasses more than just worldview and values. It covers the whole gamut from worldview and values to talents and personality. In fact, in the interest of better addressing self-awareness, it's necessary to expand the worldview-values-behaviors wheel to include two more concepts—talents and personality—as illustrated in Figure 11.

Great leaders have not only thought about their worldview and values, they have also consciously tried to uncover and identify their strengths and weaknesses, probing to understand how their personalities have wired them. Without such self-awareness, it's difficult to lead well.

People are unique. You may know two people who embrace the same worldview and the same values, but who couldn't seem more different. That difference is a function of individual talents and personality, not of worldview and values.

FIGURE 11. WHAT DRIVES LEADERS' BEHAVIORS: COMPLETING THE WHEEL

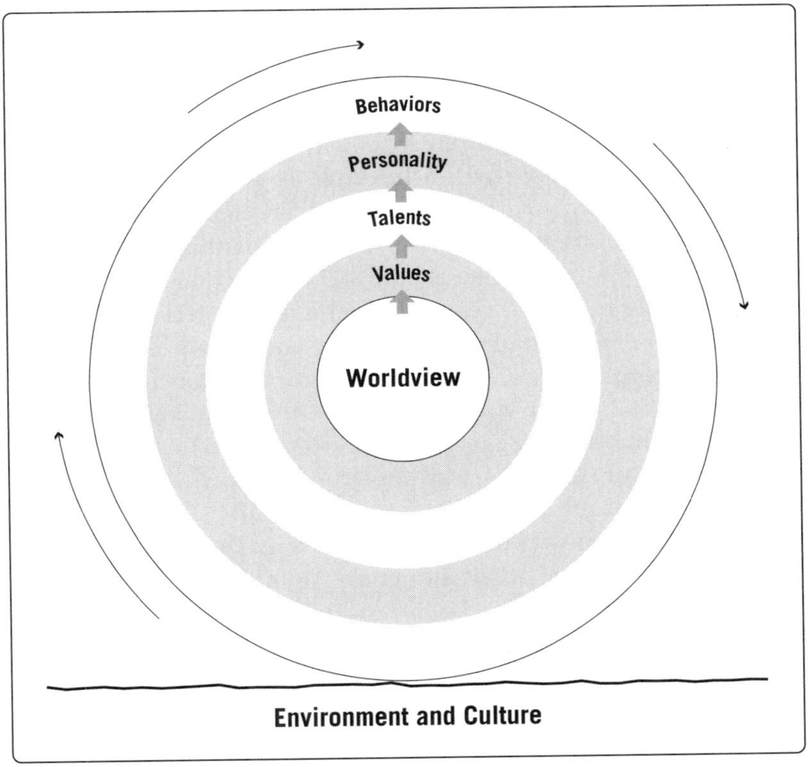

Plenty of instruments capture the subtle differences of talents and personality, but many of these differences are obvious enough without scientific assessment. One person, for example, may place a high importance on synergy and teamwork, while another may prefer independence and working alone. One may thrive on change and variety, while another needs order and predictability. For some, it's structure and precision, and for others it's fun and spontaneity; for some it may be the goal of the task and for others it may be the process of the task. Some are gifted communicators, others are not. One may be an extrovert and another an introvert; some are more abstract and others more concrete in their style of thinking.

In each case, the differences are the product of talents or personality. And, in each case, shared worldview and values may be expressed differently without altering the integrity of the worldview and values the individuals hold in common.

In Figure 11, talents and personality act as the filter for worldview and values, expressing themselves in behaviors—the outermost circle. Those behaviors don't operate in a vacuum—our behaviors are the rim that directly touches the environment and culture we operate in.

So how well is your wheel turning? That will depend on the power coming from your hub (your worldview and values), and how consciously it drives the wheel, providing momentum to resist when the environment tries to force the wheel in a direction it shouldn't go and the power to keep it going when the terrain gets rough. It will depend on the strength of the personality and talents to connect the hub to the rim; if they are weak or inappropriate for the terrain—if our talents don't match the role we're in—there will be a disconnect between the hub and the rim. And it will depend on how comfortably the rim rides on the surface of the ground—how appropriate our behaviors are for the environment we operate in.

Being able to answer the question—to know how well your wheel is turning—is an issue of self-awareness. Your level of self-awareness determines the strength and stability of the whole wheel, from worldview to behaviors (see Figure 12).

Without self-awareness, no one can change because it is impossible to understand what to change. Learning starts with self-analysis, and self-analysis leads to self-awareness. And self-awareness allows you to shape your leadership philosophy.

DEVELOPING YOUR LEADERSHIP PHILOSOPHY

If a philosophy of leadership is so crucial to a leader's effectiveness, how is it developed? Very haphazardly, to judge by the pattern most people follow. Shaped by cultural, ethnic, and family backgrounds, leadership philosophy tends to evolve unconsciously from the collective impact of the people, events, and ideas of a lifetime. Applying this hodgepodge of beliefs to leadership, people experience some that work (the good beliefs) and some that don't (the bad beliefs), and it typically takes some painful failures to confront the bad beliefs that have unconsciously been embraced. The pattern is shown in Figure 13, on page 66.

FIGURE 12. WHAT DRIVES LEADERS' BEHAVIORS: THE FINAL ELEMENT

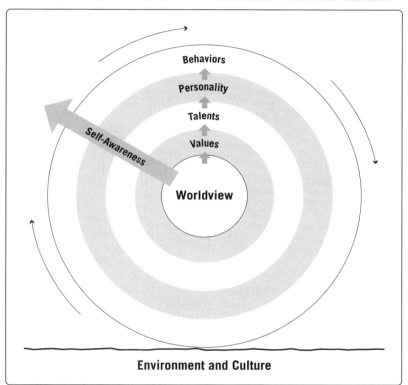

The process works, but it doesn't work well, underscoring the notion that it's what people believe falsely about leadership that weakens their leadership. There is a better way. Instead of the haphazard approach, you can start by taking a good look at what you believe about leadership and consciously define a philosophy of leadership. That good look means getting feedback from those around you to see how other people view your leadership style. It means becoming a student of leadership and using the resulting insights to consciously abandon false beliefs on leadership, to reinforce the good beliefs that are already in practice, and to embrace the good beliefs that aren't.

Unfortunately, people always have the option of reverting to old habits and assumptions—to their detriment as leaders. Instead, you need to make your own leadership development (as well as the

FIGURE 13. TYPICAL PATTERN OF LEADER BEHAVIOR AND DEVELOPMENT

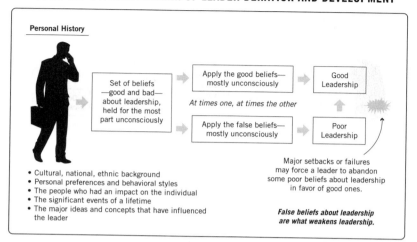

development of those you are leading) an intentional, deliberate process that is tailored to the level where you are currently operating, anticipating the next levels of leadership you are likely to move to. (Figure 14 illustrates the choice.) Development needs to be customized to your own particular leadership growth needs. This requires thought; you can't get away from the fact that your actions as a leader are shaped by your thinking as a leader.

For you as a leader, what are some applications? How do you launch yourself on this process? Here are some ideas to get you started:

- Start with a personal mission statement. View it as an ongoing process, not an item to be crossed off your to-do list. It's an enriching process; remember that your first draft will not be your final draft.

- Once you have a mission statement that you are halfway satisfied with, ask yourself, "If this is my mission statement, then what drives it? What are the values behind it? What does my mission statement tell me about what I think about ultimate authority, as well as human nature? What does it tell me about my sense of purpose and contribution?"

FIGURE 14. INTENTIONAL PATTERN OF LEADER BEHAVIOR AND DEVELOPMENT

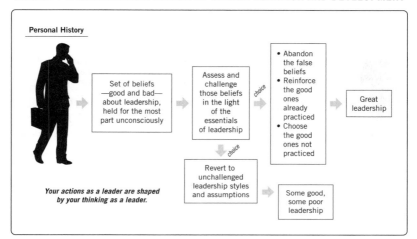

- Go back over your personal history. What impact did your family have in shaping your view of leadership? How did your ethnic and cultural background influence it? Who were the leaders you admired, and why? Who were the leaders you didn't admire, and why? What were the events and ideas that influenced you? How did all these shape your view of leadership? What do you want to keep and what do you want to reject as you bring definition to your philosophy of leadership?

- Challenge your ideas. Read books and talk with people who think differently. Your own thinking will be enlarged and your convictions challenged—thus changing or strengthening them. Either way, you will gain clarity about your core beliefs and leadership philosophy.

- Find a coach or mentor. A good coach or mentor will challenge you to ask (and answer) the tough questions. It's not just young leaders who need one; I am coming to the conclusion that the older we get, the more we need one—perhaps because we think we don't need one. Find someone who already has a clear personal worldview and who espouses values similar to your own.

- Become a student of leadership. Define what you consider to be the essentials of great leadership. Don't be afraid of borrowing ideas; at some point, they will become your own. Define and articulate your own philosophy of leadership, get outside of your company and the industry. Seek new and fresh ideas on leadership.

- Keep a journal. Get acquainted with your pen and your keyboard in a new way. Buy a good-quality notebook, and on the inside front page, give it a title such as "The Principles and Practice of Great Leadership." Below, add, "By . . ." with your name as the author. You don't have to write in it every day; when you have an idea you want to remember, an insight you want to capture, a question you want to answer, or an experience you want to learn from, write it down. Remember, leaders are not just readers—they are also writers.

If you develop yourself as leader from the inside out, the payback is huge. On the solid foundation of a thoughtful and maturing philosophy of leadership you will be able to build the personal qualities of leadership addressed in the next chapter. You won't just deal with skills and behaviors; instead, you will generate the thinking that will have the greatest impact on your leadership effectiveness. Don't focus on the outer circle; focus instead on the inner circles, and the outer circle will take care of itself. Not only will this kind of leadership shape the relationships you have with those you lead, it will also revolutionize the relationships your people have with those outside your organization—not just customers but anyone you as an organization associate with to satisfy those customers. The ripple effect is powerful.

"I will study and prepare," Abraham Lincoln once said, "and perhaps my day will come." Your day has already come—it came the moment you stepped into a leadership role.

5

THE HEART AND MIND OF THE LEADER

Embracing the Personal Qualities of Great Leadership

In *Lenin's Tomb,* a compelling account of the last days of the Soviet Empire, David Remnick gives a fascinating description of Stalin. Born in 1879 as Iosif Vissarionovich Djugashvili, he grew up with a drunkard father who beat his wife and who, mercifully, died young. As a boy, Stalin read Aleksandr Kazbeg's *The Patricide,* the story of Koba, a Georgian hero who took vengeance on its enemies. "After he read the book," Remnick writes, "Stalin demanded that all his friends call him Koba. 'That became his ideal,' wrote a childhood friend. Stalin's closest comrades in the party called him Koba—sometimes until the day he had them shot."

At the Russian Orthodox seminary where he studied, the monks called him "rude and disrespectful." His mother held high hopes that he'd enter the priesthood, and, Remnick writes, "When he visited her in 1936—by then he was already the Soviet leader and planning the Great Purge—she said, 'What a pity you did not become a priest.'"

When Stalin was forty-six, his wife, Nadezhda, left him. "He begged her to return," Remnick writes, "and at the same time had her followed by the secret police. Six years later they fought over Stalin's brutal treatment of the peasantry in Ukraine. When the row was over, Nadezhda left the room and shot herself. Her daughter, Svetlana, later said, 'I believe that my mother's death, which he took as a personal betrayal, deprived his soul of the last vestiges of human warmth.'"

Stalin lived a lonely and solitary life in the Kremlin. Much of the time, he spent listening in on the phone conversations of his advisers, who were unaware that their phones were bugged. *Pravda* was predictably effusive in the titles it conferred on Stalin: Leader and Teacher of the Workers of the World, Father of the Peoples, Wise and Intelligent Chief of the Soviet People, the Greatest Genius of All Times and Peoples, the Greatest Military Leader of All Times and Peoples, Faithful Comrade-in-Arms of Lenin, the Mountain Eagle, and Best Friend of All Children. As Remnick suggests, Stalin was obsessed with his public image:

> Stalin, who was five feet four, wanted a court portrait done showing him as a tall man with powerful hands. The painter Nalbandian complied by portraying Stalin from a flattering angle with his hands folded, powerfully, across his belly. Stalin had his other portrait painters shot and their paintings burned. Stalin rewrote the official *Short Biography of Stalin,* personally adding the passage "Stalin never allowed his work to be marred by the slightest hint of vanity, conceit, or self-adulation."

Terror, in Stalin's hands, was a well-honed instrument of power—according to Remnick, he called those who didn't use it "vegetarians." By the time he died in 1953 at the age of seventy-three, Stalin had a tally of victims that by some estimates numbered 40 million. Solzhenitsyn put the number at 60 million.

Based on this account of Stalin, what words would you use to describe him? Most probably words like ambitious, power-hungry, ruthless, heartless, and inhumane for starters—after some more thought, you might add words like insecure, vain, solitary, paranoid, isolated, and devoid of any accountability.

The interesting thing about this list is that those same words are often used to describe leaders in the marketplace. The difference is one of degree. Plenty of leaders have allowed ambition and hunger for power to take them down a path of heartless, inhumane behavior. The difference between them and Stalin has to do more with scope than intent; given access to the kind of resources Stalin had at his disposal, plenty would use them. Not everyone put in Stalin's place would act as Stalin did—far from it. But as Lord Acton pointed out over a hundred years ago, "Power tends to corrupt and absolute power corrupts absolutely." With power comes temptation, and it is much easier for leaders to give in to those temptations—to the extent their circumstances allow them to—if they are not guided by some core qualities that were clearly absent in Stalin.

In an article in the *Financial Times* (March 23–24, 1991), John Harvey-Jones (former chairman of Imperial Chemical Industries, one of Britain's largest and more venerable companies) draws some interesting conclusions on power:

> The area which caused me the most concern on a personal basis was the whole business of the effect of power on the individual. I do believe that power corrupts, and I can think of very few powerful people who have been improved by it as individuals. Positions of power are, by definition, ephemeral, while one's personal characteristics remain with one until death. Despite this, the pressures on the individual to change the attributes he or she has fought for all their lives are unremitting.
>
> As power grows, so does the chorus of flattery. Some is obvious and sickening, but much is invidious. In common with many people I am vain, and would like to like myself. I also struggle continuously to improve my own moral courage and willingness to take the unpopular ground. There are few tests for such weaknesses more profound than to be the chairman of a large international company enjoying a period of relative success.
>
> If for no other reason than this, I was glad when my time expired.

For every John Harvey-Jones, you will see many who make no pretense at resisting the temptations of power. The past decades have produced their fair share of corporate tyrants; every decade has its poster children. In the 1980s, it was people like William Klopman, chairman of Burlington Industries, whom *Fortune* (August 6, 1984) described as "unable to communicate or praise people. . . . The smartest guy I've ever met in the industry, but cold, and, some would say, ruthless. . . . Not much room for original thought at his company." Richard Rosenthal, chairman of Citizens Utilities, was described as an "incredible egomaniac . . . Cold . . . Those who have stayed with him are the kind who can get used to working with a self-proclaimed genius. . . . In dealing with Richard, you can't have an ego of your own. . . . Unbelievably litigious. . . . Fair. He has underpaid everybody equally." Fred Ackman at Superior Oil "came across as having a Napoleon complex—he had to throw his weight around. . . . Imperious. . . . Unwilling to entertain ideas that didn't fit in with his."

In the 1990s, it was Al Dunlap, who was dubbed—not very affectionately—as "Rambo in pinstripes" and "Chainsaw Al." Since the turn of the century, we have seen plenty of derailments, many of them spectacular, the majority of them united by one common characteristic: whether leaders derailed because of the way they handled corporate finances, or because of an affair, or because of inept and aggressive relational styles, they generally came to believe that they were above the laws that applied to everyone else. Power had indeed corrupted, or if not corrupted, distorted.

To uncover the qualities of truly great leaders, to uncover the heart and mind of such a leader, embark with me on a lofty exercise: painting the picture of a perfect leader, at least in terms of personal qualities. No such leader exists, of course, but we can describe the ideal, and, in doing so, we can help the real leader inch closer to the ideal.

This chapter develops the picture in terms of the pyramid shown in Figure 15, adding the building blocks one on top of another to define the perfect leader. Chapter 4 laid the foundation, describing the soul of the leader—someone with plenty of self-awareness, a clear philosophy of leadership coming from a well-defined worldview, and a clear moral compass. Without this foundation, the pyramid will crumble. With this foundation in place, however, it becomes possible to build the pyramid of personal qualities.

THE CORE OF THE PYRAMID

At the core of the pyramid, three key qualities provide structural strength: humility, focus, and care for others (see Figure 16). These three cover the broad sweep of personal qualities because they deal with the key areas of how leaders view themselves, how they view their purpose, and how they view others.

From these three, other qualities flow; but, without them, the pyramid crumbles. Everything else is an outflow of these three core qualities. Without them, little hope exists of seeing the other qualities in the pyramid.

FIGURE 15. PERSONAL QUALITIES OF GREAT LEADERSHIP: THE BASIC PYRAMID

FIGURE 16. PERSONAL QUALITIES OF GREAT LEADERSHIP: BUILDING AROUND THE CORE

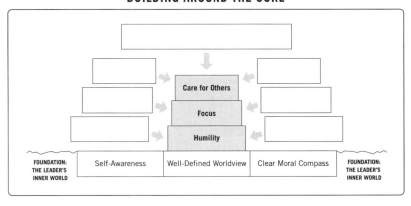

You need all three. Stalin perhaps had focus, but no humility and no care for others, to put it mildly. However, although all three need to be present, they will not manifest themselves equally all the time. Some circumstances require a stronger manifestation of one than of the others, but if it isn't latent, it won't manifest itself at all.

Humility

In our highly individualistic Western culture, humility is the surprising quality. John Wayne still casts a long shadow, even though a new generation hardly recognizes his name. Humility, however, is often misunderstood. It's not about self-deprecating insecurity; it's much more about an honest recognition of both strengths and weaknesses, reinforced by an attractive lack of preoccupation with either one. It's the antithesis of self-absorption—the recognition that "it's not about me." It's not, as someone put it, thinking less of yourself; rather, it's thinking less about yourself.

A selflessness is inherent in this kind of humility. It reflects a willingness to put the interests of the organization and of its people ahead of the leader's own interests; their success is important to the leader, and, in a very real sense, their success is the leader's success. It involves the ability to recognize the worth of others and reinforce and strengthen that worth—which is the essence of servant leadership. At the very least, the great leaders' success does not come at the expense of their people's success.

Humility is rare in leaders, but when it's there, it's powerful. It's powerful because it's disarming. Early in my career, one of my bosses in France was brought in to replace my existing boss, who headed up the French division of this nonprofit organization. What unfolded was one of the most vivid examples of humility—from both parties—I have ever witnessed. This would normally have been a confrontation of two strong leaders posturing for the same position, but the one who was being replaced—whose entrepreneurial approach was perceived by the corporate leadership as no longer appropriate for the growth needs of the French division—set out, as he put it, to "prove himself wrong," despite very real misgivings. And the one coming in came in with a spirit of servant leadership; as he put it, "There's always room for another servant." The transition turned out to be the best of its kind that the organization had ever seen, thanks to the humility of the two leaders involved. Both put the interests of the organization above their own, and in the process their stature as leaders was substantially enhanced.

The antithesis of humility is arrogance. When Leona Helmsley quipped that only the little people pay taxes, she betrayed an arrogance that in her mind gave her license to live by different rules. The laws that applied to the "little people" didn't apply to her, though in the end, to her surprise, they did.

When I was working for a Dutch brokerage firm, running the office in eastern France, I had a counterpart in Paris who led, somewhat to my envy, a thriving and prosperous operation. On one of my visits to Paris, I happened to be in his office when he pulled off one

FIGURE 17. PERSONAL QUALITIES OF GREAT LEADERSHIP: BUILDING AROUND HUMILITY

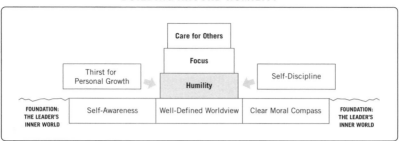

of his more spectacular deals. To those of us assembled with him, he proclaimed, *"Maintenant on sait qu'on connait bien notre métier"* (Now we know we have mastered our business). Within months, however, he and his staff experienced several setbacks, and one year later the office was closed down, my colleague and his office a casualty of his arrogance. It was sobering. Perhaps Intel's Andy Grove told the simple truth in his title—*Only the Paranoid Survive!* Or, perhaps, the humble survive.

Humility rests firmly on the foundation of self-awareness. If self-awareness and the enforced realism it imposes aren't part of the foundation, it's hard to imagine humility ever becoming a solid piece of the core structure. It's too easy to believe your own press clippings, and, the higher you go, the more people crowd around to reinforce those press clippings. It's easier than anyone imagines for a naked emperor to be convinced he's fully clothed. He just needs enough people telling him so.

Humility generates two qualities: a thirst for personal growth and a healthy dose of self-discipline, as Figure 17 illustrates.

Thirst for growth. Humility breeds a thirst for personal growth. It requires a certain measure of humility to recognize what you don't know and an equal measure to want to keep on learning. That's what great leaders do—they never stop learning. They constantly look for ways to improve themselves, willing to learn from any source available. As Lincoln said, we can learn just as well from a bad example as we can from a good one—a bad one simply tells us what not to do.

This thirst for personal growth suggests a commitment to lifelong learning, which, given the pace of change we experience today, is a necessity rather than a luxury. My father spent his entire career with one institution (the British equivalent of the State Department), as did my father-in-law (with what was then called US Steel). Today, some estimate that the average number of careers people are likely to experience is seven—not just employers, but careers. If that is even only half true, it still requires constantly retooling as a commitment to lifelong learning. If that is true for everyone, how much more so for leaders.

One of the great tests of thirst for growth is openness to feedback. I tell my clients that feedback is a gift, though sometimes when they receive it, their first instinct is anything but gratitude. It is nonetheless a gift for any of us, the unpleasant as well as the pleasant, because it tells us something about ourselves that we don't know or don't want to face, but need to know and face. We all need someone to tell us when we are walking around with spinach in our teeth.

Embracing and seeking feedback is thus a hallmark of great leadership, and, when leaders start modeling a receptiveness to feedback, they begin to create a culture where development can take root. One of the leaders I worked with attributed the turnaround in her executive team to the time when she asked them to discuss, without her presence, what they wanted her to keep doing, stop doing, and start doing. After their discussion, she returned, and when they gave her the feedback from their collective conclusions, there were some pleasant surprises and some unpleasant. One of the pleasant and significant surprises—though it only emerged over time—was their growing willingness to follow her example and embrace the value of feedback for their development as leaders.

Feedback is not always graciously given, but great leaders take it anyway. At one point during the Civil War, Lincoln issued an authorization to the War Department that was immediately countermanded by his secretary of war, Edwin Stanton. The messenger who relayed this information told Lincoln that Stanton had not only countermanded the authorization but had also called the president "a damn fool" for issuing it. "Did Stanton say I was a damn fool?" Lincoln asked. When he was told that he did (and that he actually repeated it), Lincoln responded, "If Stanton said I was a damn fool, then I must be one, for he is nearly always right and generally says what he means. I will step over and see him." Great leaders welcome feedback, whatever the form it takes.

Self-discipline. Humility breeds a thirst for self-discipline as well. Humility recognizes that greatness requires work, and work requires self-discipline. Great leaders work hard, and, most of all, they work hard on themselves. "In reading the lives of great men," Truman once said, "I found that the first victory they won was over themselves. . . . Self-discipline with all of them came first."

This self-discipline takes many forms, because different leaders wrestle with different temptations. Self-discipline is about choices. We can choose to focus on strengthening our weaknesses, or we can choose to focus on giving greater expression to our strengths; every voice around us urges us to focus on our weaknesses, and it requires self-discipline to keep working through our strengths—the better but harder choice. Self-discipline is about controlling our appetites, whatever they may be. Self-discipline is about living consistently with our worldview and philosophy of leadership, applying principle above preference, thus creating a consistency of leadership behavior that the people we lead can trust and rely on.

Shakespeare captures the need to exercise self-discipline well in *Henry V*; the young king, new to the throne, realizes that he can't engage in the lifestyle he reveled in before his ascension. In *A Distant Mirror*, historian Barbara Tuchman describes him entering "upon a reign of stern virtue and heroic conquest," with all the energy of "a reformed rake." Early on in *Henry V*, the Archbishop of Canterbury reflects on the young king's former lifestyle:

> His addiction was to courses vain;
> His companies unlettered, rude and shallow;
> His hours filled up with riots, banquets, sports;
> And never noted in him any study,
> Any retirement, any sequestration
> From open haunts and popularity.

The change that overcame the king when his father died, the Archbishop muses, was nothing short of remarkable:

> The breath no sooner left his father's body
> But that his wildness, mortified in him,
> Seemed to die too: yea, at that very moment,
> Consideration, like an angel, came,
> And whipped the offending Adam out of him . . .
> Never was such a sudden scholar made;

Never came reformation in a flood,
With such a heady current, scouring faults . . .
As in this king.

Leadership brings responsibility, and responsibility requires self-discipline—something the young "King Harry" figured out very quickly. Perhaps he had read the words of Gregory the Great, a pope who preceded him by more than eight hundred years: "He who is required by the necessity of his position to speak the highest things is compelled by the same necessity to exemplify them."

Focus

The next block in the core of the pyramid is focus. Focus is about passion, but passion doesn't mean extrovert exuberance. A leader can be an introvert and still be a passionate, focused leader. It has to do with perseverance more than personality.

One of my friends at one time had a sign outside his office door that read, "Keep the main thing the main thing." Someone, however, had changed it so that it read, "Keep the 23 main things the 23 main things." The tongue-in-cheek addition highlighted how difficult maintaining focus really is, and yet focus is one of the core qualities of great leaders. Churchill once observed that a bulldog's snout is slanted backwards so the dog can keep breathing without letting go. That image appealed to him, and it captures well the nature of focus. Jim Collins identified this quality in *Good to Great* as a tenaciousness for the cause that knows no deterrent.

Focus is the ability to articulate a clear sense of direction and to maintain that direction—both of the leader and of those who are led. Without focus, thinking will tend to diffuse and action become inconsistent. With focus, the ability to think and the ability to act are given context and substance (see Figure 18).

The ability to think. Great leaders are disciplined thinkers. They are not, as the philosopher William James observed, like those who "merely rearrange their prejudices." They have about them a transcendent common sense, an ability to apply practical reason to the challenge they are facing.

And they can do this under pressure because they've figured out their response before the crises and the challenges come—they did it when they defined their philosophy of leadership and the moral com-

FIGURE 18. PERSONAL QUALITIES OF GREAT LEADERSHIP: BUILDING AROUND FOCUS

pass they would travel by, as suggested in Figure 19. Crises test not so much our reactions as the thinking we put into preparing for them. Reagan could tell Gorbachev to "tear this wall down" because he had done his thinking first. When Reagan was widely criticized for laying a wreath in a German graveyard where several SS officers were buried, he explained to the press that, when he invited Chancellor Kohl to lay a wreath at the tomb of the Unknown Soldier in Washington, he had promised to do the same at a gravesite of Kohl's choosing—he was going to keep his word.

The fact that we have brains doesn't mean that we think well any more than having ears means that we listen well. Whether the thinking required of us is innovation, problem solving, or practical wisdom, it is hard work. Roy Thomson, a Canadian entrepreneur who created a powerful and far-flung publishing empire, wrote in his autobiography, *After I Was Sixty:*

> Thinking is work. In the early stages of a man's career it is very hard work. When a difficult decision or problem arises, how easy it is, after looking at it superficially, to give up thinking about it. It is easy to put it from one's mind. It is easy to decide that it is insoluble, or that something will turn up to help us. . . . If one wants to be successful, one must think; one must think until it hurts. . . . There are few people indeed who are prepared to perform this arduous and tiring work.

Just as important as the ability to think is the ability to stimulate thinking. Great leaders think with discipline, and they engage others in sound thinking, practical reasoning, lively imagination, and transcendent common sense. In *Apollo 13*, Gene Krantz was unrelenting in pushing people to find creative solutions, insisting "Failure is not

FIGURE 19. PERSONAL QUALITIES OF GREAT LEADERSHIP: FURTHER BUILDING AROUND FOCUS

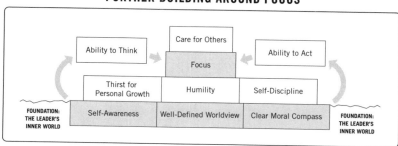

an option!" He didn't come up with the answers himself, but without his ability to drive reasoned and creative problem solving, there would likely have been no survivors.

One of my earlier mentors had a tremendous impact on his mentees by forcing us to think; he challenged our often woolly and unquestioned assumptions and pushed us to look at them differently. It was invaluable, but not always comfortable. As Don Marquis, a humorist from the early 1900s, once commented, "If you make people think they're thinking, they'll love you; but if you really make them think, they'll hate you." We didn't always appreciate our mentor's challenges, but, with time, we did.

The ability to act. The ability to act is another outgrowth of focus, and it is intimately tied to the ability to think. "The origin of action," Aristotle wrote, "is choice, and the origin of choice is apposite and purposive reasoning." The Greeks did much to codify reasoning, but the best of them never argued for reasoning divorced from action.

One of Lincoln's challenges during the Civil War was finding generals who had the courage to act. At one point, exasperated with General George McClellan's indecisiveness, Lincoln wrote him a one-sentence letter:

> My Dear McClellan:
>
> If you are not using the army, I should like to borrow it for a short while.
>
> Yours respectfully,
>
> Abraham Lincoln

When he picked General Ulysses S. Grant as commander of the East, after a string of inept generals, he told him he wanted a commander "to take responsibility and act." A controversial choice, Lincoln defended him, because, he said, "He fights."

Thought without action is stagnant. Great leaders go from thought to decision to action. At some point, often sooner rather than later, they are required to take responsible, timely, and decisive action. While risk is involved, good leaders conclude that the risk of inaction is greater.

Many leaders lament the lack of initiative they see in their people. The truth is that this lack of initiative says more about the leader than it does about the people. Leaders unwittingly stifle initiative in many ways, but mostly by micromanaging decisions, rescinding decisions others have made, and demanding constant accountability for every decision. Such leaders use meetings as a decision-making forum and as a bludgeon to follow up on the way decisions are carried out. They kill initiative and stifle the ability to act.

Care for Others

The final core brick is care for others—which is by no means the same as being nice to others. Great leaders genuinely care for the people they lead, but they may not be nice to them. Sherman was one of the most demanding generals of the Civil War, imposing sudden and grueling marches in the middle of the night for a surprise attack on Confederate forces. And that was the very reason his soldiers loved him: he cared about what mattered most to them—their survival. He led them in a way that made survival a greater likelihood.

What makes Dorothy in *The Wizard of Oz* such an endearing figure is this underlying care for the motley crew she recruited and led to the Emerald City. She didn't recruit them to her mission (getting back to Kansas); instead, she figured out what they wanted and how what she was doing could help each of them find what they were looking for—a brain for the Scarecrow, a heart for the Tin Man, and courage for the Cowardly Lion. Had she not exhibited that kind of concern, it's unlikely they would have joined her.

Care for others generates sacrifice for others and connection with others, as shown in Figure 20.

Sacrifice for others. Care for others will be expressed in some form by a willingness to sacrifice for the benefit of those we lead. We typically

FIGURE 20. PERSONAL QUALITIES OF GREAT LEADERSHIP: BUILDING AROUND CARE FOR OTHERS

think of sacrifice as something heroic and final, such as an officer throwing himself on a hand grenade to protect his soldiers, or the Polish priest in the concentration camp offering to be shot in the place of the father of four. And it might be.

But, leaders' sacrifice for others is usually a daily and cumulative effort focused on the success and interests of the people in their charge. It's translating care into action, putting the interests of those being led ahead of one's own, demonstrating what is best described as servant leadership. This kind of sacrifice devotes time, thought, and effort to bringing out everyone's best. It requires an intentionality that takes time and effort, and the sacrifice of that time and effort is one of the greatest expressions of care that we can offer to the people we lead.

Connection with others. Care for others is also the ability to connect with people through emotion and empathy, a quality known as emotional intelligence. This concept was popularized and expanded by Daniel Goleman (see, for example, *Working with Emotional Intelligence*). Leaders who have this quality have learned that their people are moved more by emotion than by logic; and, because good leaders tap into not only their own emotions but also those of their constituents, they connect. They understand how their people feel; this ability to empathize is in fact one of the corner pieces of emotional intelligence.

One of Lincoln's strengths was his disarming empathy. He was unusual among opponents to slavery in his unwillingness to condemn slave owners. "They are just what we would be in their situation. If slavery did not now exist amongst them, they would not

FIGURE 21. PERSONAL QUALITIES OF GREAT LEADERSHIP: ADDING THE CAPSTONE

introduce it. If it did now exist amongst us, we should not instantly give it up." As he said in his second Inaugural Address, "Both read the same Bible, and pray to the same God; and each invokes His aid against the other . . . Let us not judge," he concluded, "that we be not judged." He had the ability to condemn the practice and yet show extraordinary compassion and empathy for those practicing it.

Some leaders exercise this emotional intelligence without a genuine care for the people they lead. They have the ability to connect with others at a deeper emotional level, but they don't exercise this strength in the best interests of their people. In the end, they manipulate them, and it isn't long before their actions are perceived as such.

COURAGE: THE CAPSTONE OF THE PYRAMID

Courage is the capstone—without which, none of the other qualities will be fully expressed (see Figure 21).

One of the great battles of antiquity was fought in 480 B.C. at a narrow pass in Greece called Thermopylae. It was no more than twenty yards wide, the sea on one side and Mount Kallidromos, whose cliffs towered five thousand feet above the pass, on the other. It was a well-chosen spot, because the defending Greeks were outrageously outnumbered—a mixed, undisciplined band of seven thousand from several city-states that bickered and fought among themselves . . . no match for the opposing army, led by the young

Persian King Xerxes and, according to the Greek historian Herodotus, three million strong.

At the heart of the ill-fated band of Greeks were three hundred Spartans led Leonidas. They took their stand in the pass, and for two days, they repulsed wave after wave of the Persian war machine. "Then, disastrously, the Greeks were betrayed," as Os Guinness describes it in *The Call*:

> By night a traitor led the Persians over the cliffs so that at daybreak Leonidas and his men were surrounded. The pass had been sold. The game was up. Death was coming as surely as the dawn. Dismissing most of his army, Leonidas led his own three hundred Spartans and a few others to a little mound from which they could make their last desperate stand and hold back the oncoming avalanche. There the little band fought to the last man and died. When their swords were gone, according to Herodotus, they fought with their hands and teeth. But before they died, they sent home the stirring message that became their epitaph: "Stranger, tell the Spartans that we behaved as they would wish us to, and are buried here."

Thermopylae was a defeat that became a victory. Its significance is felt even today, because the stand at Thermopylae rallied Greece to defend itself against the Persian army and to go on to defeat it soundly at Salamis and Platae. Within thirty years, Athens became one of the most influential cities this world has known; it was the birthplace of democracy, and to it we trace the roots of our democratic institutions.

Courage takes many forms and has many expressions. At Thermopylae, courage meant knowing the odds were insurmountable and facing them anyway. "Real courage," Harper Lee wrote in *To Kill a Mockingbird*, "is when you know you're licked before you begin, but you begin anyway and see it through no matter what." It's the willingness to face undeniable odds and keep going. "The time is always right," Martin Luther King Jr. said, "to do what is right," even if the odds are not in favor of it turning out well. As he later said, "The ultimate measure of a man is not where he stands in moments of comfort and convenience, but where he stands at times of challenge and controversy." At times of challenge and controversy the outcome seldom looks good, but courage keeps us pressing on anyway. As humorist Garrison Keillor said, "Sometimes you need to look reality in the eye, and deny it."

Courage is acting on principle, not poll. At the outset of World War II, 80 percent of the British population favored peace with Germany; had Churchill listened to the polls, we would now be seeing a very different Europe. Harry Truman, who made one of the toughest decisions a leader was ever faced with (using the first atomic bomb) and who made one of the most far-sighted decisions after the war (establishing the Marshall Plan for European recovery), once said, "I wonder how far Moses would have gone if he had taken a poll in Egypt." Churchill said, "Nothing is more dangerous . . . than to live in the temperamental atmosphere of a Gallup Poll—always feeling one's pulse and taking one's temperature." His response to the notion that leaders should keep their ears to the ground was that "the British nation will find it very hard to look up to the leaders who are detected in that somewhat ungainly posture." Whatever their context, great leaders are willing to take the difficult and courageous decisions, whatever the prevailing winds and whatever the personal cost.

In great leaders, the courage to press on in spite of the polls is matched by the courage to accept responsibility for their mistakes. The myth of the perfect leader is still pervasive, but genuinely great leaders make, and admit to, mistakes. When Grant made a military decision that Lincoln thought was ill-advised (a decision Grant vindicated with a spectacular victory at Vicksburg), Lincoln told Grant, "I feared it was a mistake. I now wish to make the personal acknowledgment that you were right, and I was wrong."

Courage is also the willingness to make sacrifices for those we lead. It takes courage to place their interests above our own. It takes courage to invest in their lives; personal and professional growth can be a messy business, and it takes a measure of courage to roll up our sleeves and thrust our hands in the dirt.

Selecting strong leaders takes courage. When Lincoln appointed his three Republican rivals in the primaries to his cabinet—William Henry Seward, Salmon Chase, and Edward Bates, all three better educated and perhaps better qualified for the office—he took the political community by surprise and was roundly condemned for a naive and foolish move. But, as his secretary, John Nicolay, later wrote, Lincoln's "first decision was one of great courage and self-reliance." Great leaders have the courage to select talent greater than their own.

Courage is also the willingness to look inside. It's the courage to acknowledge weaknesses, to be authentic, and to ask oneself the tough questions. It's the courage to face unresolved questions and perhaps live with them. It's the courage to accept feedback and examine it honestly. It's the courage to avoid settling for simplistic answers and to look within in an effort to shape what is seen without. It's what Robert Quinn's *Building the Bridge as You Walk on It* calls "the fundamental state of leadership," which is the antithesis of the "normal state, refusing to change while the universe changes around us, [which] is ultimately to choose slow death." To enter the fundamental state of leadership "is to reverse the process by making deep change. . . . When we are in this state, we become more purpose-centered, internally driven, other-focused, and externally open." It takes courage to embark on this journey within.

Courage, in the end, is a function of commitment. Courage is greatest when stakes are highest. That's why, as German military theorist Carl von Clausewitz pointed out, boldness becomes rarer the higher the rank. The only way we will exercise courage is if we believe firmly enough in the cause that requires it. If we do, we will act on principles, not polls. We will be willing to be unpopular, we will be willing to acknowledge our mistakes, we will be willing to roll up our sleeves, we will be willing to risk hiring talent greater than our own.

Courage gains strength when it's collective. It's much easier to be courageous when those around us encourage us to be courageous. The Cowardly Lion in the *Wizard of Oz* would never have overcome his fears if he hadn't had some people around who refused to let him give in to his fears. Courage is easier if it's reinforced. Also, some acts of courage may be acts of folly; we need people around us who can help us distinguish courage from folly, and who, when courage is called for, don't let us give in to our fears.

When I was a young child, I heard a radio play about four climbers caught in a blizzard in the Swiss Alps. With great difficulty, they managed to pitch a tent, and there they sat hoping to ride out the storm. But it never let up, and they eventually realized they had no chance of surviving. They began opening up to each other. One shared his thoughts about his disappointing marriage, and then one said: "I always wanted to emigrate to New Zealand, but I never had the guts." His three companions protested, saying, "What do you mean, you didn't have the guts? You're the most courageous climber of us all." He silenced them with these words: "There's short-term guts and long-term guts. I've got short-term guts."

It's long-term guts we need as leaders.

FIGURE 22. PERSONAL QUALITIES OF GREAT LEADERSHIP:
THE MORTAR

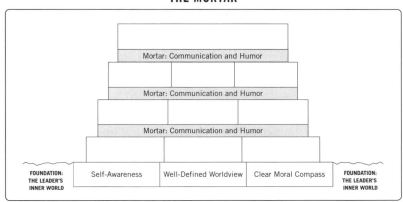

FIGURE 22. PERSONAL QUALITIES OF GREAT LEADERSHIP:
THE MORTAR

THE MORTAR: COMMUNICATION AND HUMOR

Every layer of the leadership pyramid needs to be held in place. In practice, the mortar that keeps them together is communication and humor, as shown in Figure 22.

Communication. Communication is the ability to articulate ideas clearly and concisely. It's the ability to paint pictures with words. It's the art of symbolism.

Dead Poets Society is a movie about a teacher at a New England private boarding school. New to the school, his gift and mission is to challenge the assumptions imposed on the students by their background and surroundings and to see possibilities that those assumptions blind them to. Carpe diem (seize the day) becomes the theme, and he launches the theme by taking them to a venerable hallway filled with trophies and group photos of the school's alumni. He directs them to the earliest photos, where all those posing are now long dead, and tells his students to listen to what their predecessors are telling them—which, of course, is carpe diem. He could have delivered the message from the front of the classroom, but the symbolic backdrop he chose stirred many of his students to listen with a more attentive ear.

Based on a true story, *Remember the Titans* is a captivating movie about an African American hired as the football coach for a high school in the throes of desegregation. He has the daunting challenge of creating a new team out of a previously all-white team and a previously all-black team. At one point during training camp he makes the players go on a grueling early-morning run that brings them to the battlefield of Gettysburg just as dawn is breaking. With his audience leaning on each other from exhaustion, and with the backdrop of history and the sunrise breaking through the trees, he delivers a simple but stirring message on reconciling their differences and coming together as a team. It was a message he could have delivered between practice sessions on the field, but its power came from the symbolism of the context he engineered.

Important though it is, however, symbolism is not the key to communication. Substance is the key. Substance creates authenticity. To communicate well you have to have ideas. Reagan was called the great communicator, but he was able to communicate because he had clear ideas. Before he was elected to the presidency, he asked Richard Allen (his first national security adviser) if he would like to hear his theory on the Cold War. "Some people think I'm simplistic," he went on, "but there's a difference between being simplistic and being simple. My theory of the Cold War is that we win and they lose. What do you think about that?" Richard Allen recalled: "I'd worked for Nixon and Goldwater and many others, and I'd heard a lot about . . . détente and the need to 'manage the Cold War,' but never did I hear a politician put the goal so starkly." The clarity of Reagan's ideas made them easy to communicate. Without clear ideas, the gift of communication is mere babble.

William Wilberforce was considered one of the best orators of his time. From his election to Parliament in 1780 at age twenty-one, he was a rising star. His career was indeed memorable, and his oratory was captivating. But what made him remarkable was not so much his oratory as his ideas—and his undeniable commitment to those ideas.

Wilberforce was the driving factor behind the abolition of the slave trade and, later, of slavery itself within the British colonies. Animated by a strong faith, physically unprepossessing, beset by poor health—and a fierce opposition—he nonetheless battled for the abolition of the slave trade for more than twenty years.

Then he put his energies and considerable communication skills to the task of outlawing slavery itself. Three days before he died in 1833, Parliament vindicated his efforts by passing a law abolishing slavery in all British colonies. Lincoln later wrote, "I have not allowed myself to forget . . . the abolition of the slave trade by Great Britain. . . .

Schoolboys know that Wilberforce . . . helped move that cause forward."

In November 1863, two speeches were made at Gettysburg. One lasted two hours and was delivered by renowned orator Edward Everett. The other lasted about ten minutes. The moving remarks delivered by Lincoln, who by the standards of his day was anything but a good speaker, are the ones we remember, and we remember them because of their succinct and eloquent expression of great ideas.

Churchill was considered a great orator, and every time he spoke in the House of Commons, it was full. But he was above all a man of ideas, and he spent hours preparing his speeches. His valet once heard him talking in the bath and went to see if he needed anything. "No— I'm just addressing the House of Commons," was the reply. He worked hard at his craft because he believed in the ideas it conveyed.

Sense of humor. A sense of humor suggests two qualities: the ability to not take oneself too seriouslyand even laugh at oneself, and the ability to change moods with levity.

The ability to laugh at oneself may well be the greatest sign of authenticity. There's something appealing about people whose humor is mostly directed at themselves and not at others. Self-deprecating humor is actually a sign of strength, not lack of confidence: it takes a secure leader to acknowledge mistakes, foibles, and weaknesses, and it takes an even more secure leader to be able to laugh at them.

A sense of humor also involves the ability to change moods. "Among those whom I like or admire," poet W. H. Auden once said, "I can find no common denominator; but among those whom I love, I can: all of them made me laugh." And perhaps that's the difference between the great leaders we admire and the ones we love: the ones we love make us laugh, and, because they make us laugh, we want to be around them. As Reagan went into the operating room after a failed attempt on his life, he quipped to the doctors treating him, "I hope you are all Republicans." We are drawn to someone who in the heat of the moment can lighten our emotions.

In *Time* magazine (July 4, 2005), Doris Kearns Goodwin describes Lincoln as possessing "a remarkable sense of humor and a gift for storytelling that allowed him to defuse tensions and relax his colleagues at difficult moments. Many of his stories, taken from his seemingly limitless stock, were directly applicable to a point being argued. Many were self-deprecatory, all were hilarious. When he began one of them, his 'eyes would sparkle with fun,' one old-timer remembered, 'and when he reached the point in his narrative which invariably evoked the laughter of the crowd, nobody's enjoyment was greater than his.'"

Churchill had an extraordinary knack for injecting levity into awkward moments. At one point during the war when he was visiting Canada, he was invited to a luncheon in his honor. The host, knowing Churchill's taste for whiskey, asked him if he wanted one. He didn't normally drink that early in the day, but without much persuasion, he accepted. To keep him company, the other guests at the table also accepted—except for a local bishop, who stood up and indignantly proclaimed, "I would rather commit adultery than drink whiskey." When Churchill heard this, he called out to the young lady serving them, who was retreating to the kitchen, "Wait, wait! Come back! I didn't know there was a choice!" Albeit at the bishop's expense, humor averted an embarrassing moment.

Churchill managed to conjure up humor in the most contrary circumstances. At one point during the Battle of Britain, he and his valet were trapped in a private railroad car. With frustration and impatience growing by the minute, he turned to his valet and asked him to calculate the interior cubic feet of the rail car. They then calculated Churchill's lifetime consumption of brandy up to that time and converted the amount into cubic feet. Churchill then instructed his valet to take a red map marker and draw a line on the wall all the way around the interior of the car to reflect the volume of his consumption. The line came to about a third of the way up the wall; as he gazed at it, he muttered, "So much to do, and so little time."

THE PYRAMID IN PRACTICE

So there you have it: the ideal leader—set on a solid foundation, with a core of humility, focus, and care for others; strengthened with qualities related to each; capped with courage; and cemented with solid communication skills and a vibrant sense of humor. Figure 23 presents the whole picture.

Of course, you and I know that no single leader captures all these characteristics perfectly and fully, but has anyone come close? Yes— all the leaders we admire for the right reasons. Lincoln, obviously, of whom Sherman, not someone given to superlatives, said, "Of all the men I ever met, he seemed to possess more of the elements of great-

FIGURE 23. THE WHOLE PYRAMID OF GREAT LEADERSHIP

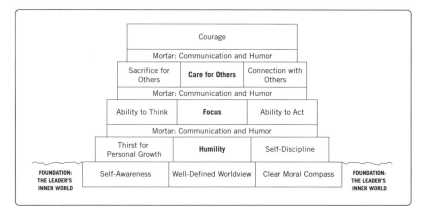

ness, combined with goodness, than any other." We can add John Adams, George Washington, William Wilberforce, Winston Churchill, Mahatma Gandhi, Mother Theresa. Others certainly deserve consideration—leaders like Elizabeth I of England, whose reign was critical in laying the foundations for both the British Empire and the spread of democracy, and Harry Truman, whose presidency did much to shape the second half of the most tumultuous century the world has ever lived through. Others deserve mention because they excelled in certain aspects of great leadership; in the marketplace, we can find at least a few of these qualities in people like Andrew Carnegie, Henry Ford, Tom Watson, Alfred Sloane, and Sam Walton, who, flawed though they were, pioneered business models that did much to shape the economic landscape of the twentieth century.

These examples are familiar public figures. Invisible to us are many others who exercised the same qualities but never received a mention in recorded history. Perhaps that lack of visibility makes these qualities all the more worthy, and perhaps most important, tells us we too can exercise these qualities. And if there is one place where these qualities need to be exercised, it is in the marketplace, because it's in the marketplace that much of leadership is exercised. As we pursue these qualities, we may not achieve widespread recognition, but we can achieve greatness nonetheless—especially if we add competence—the subject of the next chapters—to character.

PART III

COMPETENCE IN LEADERSHIP

Knowledge, Skill, and Talent

6

THE THREE DIMENSIONS OF LEADERSHIP

Finding the Right Leadership Mix
for the Right Leadership Role

Theologian Francis Schaeffer once compared truth to a table: we tend to stake out a point on the table and call it truth, when in reality the whole table is truth. This isn't an argument for the relativity of truth; it simply states that truth is larger than most of us conceive it.

The same can be said of leadership. If we compare leadership to a table, most of us stake out a point on the table and define leadership in terms of that particular point, when in reality leadership is as large as the whole table. Each of us is drawn to a particular point on the table, usually because that's where our leadership style sits most comfortably. We may also stake out that point to emulate a leader we admire or in reaction to an abuse of leadership we have witnessed or experienced.

And, of course, the rest of the table is not empty; every point is filled with strong voices calling compellingly for their particular leadership style. To make sense of this cacophony, start by distinguishing the three dimensions of leadership alluded to earlier: *organizational* leadership, *operational* leadership, and *people* leadership. Most of the confusion in leadership turns out to be confusion over these three dimensions.

MIKE'S STORY

If ever there was a spectacular fall, it was Mike's. It was brutal and painful, but it was spectacular because it had seemed so unlikely.

With a highly rated engineering degree and an even more respectable MBA, Mike was for all appearances a man destined for successful leadership. He was well credentialed, and he was well liked. Charismatic and attractive, he was adept at making genuine friends of the people that mattered. He wasn't manipulative; on the contrary, he had a reputation for high standards of integrity. People trusted him and he had a strong following. And, of course, he got the job done. He was a nuts-and-bolts guy who came up with surprising results. If his results surprised some, the promotions that came at regular and frequent intervals surprised no one.

Over time, the luster began to fade. It wasn't for want of trying. With every promotion, Mike was working harder and longer, but he seemed to meet the expectations of his staff and superiors less and less. By the time he became head of one of the company's flagship business units, he was irritable and demanding. He was working long hours, and, without actually saying it, he clearly indicated that he expected everyone else to keep the same long hours. Complaints of micromanagement multiplied, and an exodus of good people began and then accelerated. The reservoir of goodwill he had built up was rapidly draining, and his anticipated spot at the top of the organization didn't seem quite so guaranteed.

The inevitable happened. Mistakes, miscues, and misjudgments multiplied and became increasingly difficult to overlook. The harder Mike tried to avoid making them, the less he seemed able to. He talked to some people he trusted, mostly outside the company; but, sadly, no one could help him because no one understood what was going on. However, nobody missed the erosion of people's confidence in him. His bosses' focus shifted from helping Mike to replacing him. The business unit he was leading was too important to wait for him to change, which didn't seem likely anyway. Mike sensed the shift, and his defensive reaction verged on paranoia. His defensiveness, unfortunately, only made it harder for him to change.

Mike's problem was not an issue of character. It was an issue of competence—of leadership competence. Given his many attributes, his competence was never questioned, by others or by him. But it was nonetheless at the root of his difficulties: he hadn't understood how his leadership responsibilities had changed with each promotion. He had carried on doing what he'd done all along: he didn't realize that success at one level could spell failure at another.

DISTINGUISHING THE THREE DIMENSIONS OF LEADERSHIP

A first leadership experience is typically operational, and Mike's was no exception. Even his educational background had an operational focus; he was an engineer, and his MBA didn't significantly change that orientation, since MBAs focus mainly on operational and financial management. So neither education nor experience prepared him to assume the leadership challenges his promotions were giving him. He continued exercising operational leadership in an environment that increasingly demanded organizational leadership, and people leadership was something he'd never given a lot of thought to. Mike's experience was quite different from the balanced presence of all three shown in Figure 24; his operational leadership circle was disproportionately large, and the other two were disproportionately small, bordering on nonexistent.

To understand what was going on with Mike, it's necessary to understand the meaning of organizational leadership, operational leadership, and people leadership.

- *Organizational leadership* has to do with the effectiveness and relevance of the organization. The focus is primarily external. This is the ship's captain and the senior officers on the bridge and at the helm, looking out ahead, adjusting to weather conditions, and relaying that information to the engineers.

- *Operational leadership* has to do with the efficiency and responsiveness of the organization's operations. The focus is primarily internal. These are the engineers, the cooks, and anyone else whose role contributes to the smooth and efficient operation of the ship.

FIGURE 24. THE THREE DIMENSIONS OF LEADERSHIP

- *People leadership* has to do with the productivity of the individuals working in the organization—from the captain to the engineer to the deckhands. When people leadership is exercised well, leaders look for ways to bring out the best in the people they're responsible for.

What happened to Mike? He had fallen into a trap that many fall into as promotions come and responsibilities increase. He had failed to understand the shift in balance as he moved from operational leadership to organizational leadership. He was working in the business, not on the business.

THE RELATIONSHIP BETWEEN ORGANIZATIONAL LEADERSHIP AND OPERATIONAL LEADERSHIP

In an ideal world, the normal and healthy career path of a leader typically involves a decreasing proportion of operational leadership and an increasing proportion of organizational leadership. If Mike's career

FIGURE 25. THE TRADE-OFF BETWEEN ORGANIZATIONAL LEADERSHIP AND OPERATIONAL LEADERSHIP

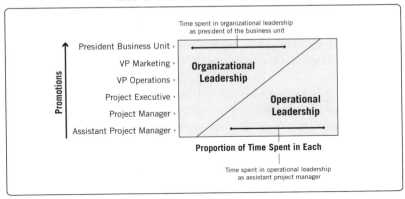

FIGURE 26. HOW MIKE REALLY SPENT HIS TIME

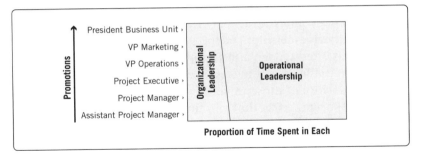

path had been healthy, the changing mix between the two would have looked something like the diagram in Figure 25. By the time he became president of the business unit, he would have been spending about the same amount of time in organizational leadership as he would have spent in operational leadership as an assistant project manager.

The focus of his position shifted, but Mike never shifted with it. His focus remained on operational leadership, because that's what he understood and that's where he felt comfortable. His leadership balance looked more like that shown in Figure 26.

Mike did what most people do. People get promoted because they're good at what they do, and because they're good they keep doing it even when their new responsibilities require something different. They work harder, because the scope of their work has expanded—instead of overseeing one project, they are now overseeing six—and they assume they can give the same oversight to the six that they gave to the one. This unfounded optimism, in Mike's case, resulted in severe consequences for both the organization and his career.

The difference between a frontline manager and a CEO or business unit leader is enormous in virtually every aspect of the work—the time frame they need to make decisions within, the priorities they need to focus on, and the skills they need to succeed in their roles. The time frame, for example, that shaped Mike's decisions as an assistant project manager would most likely be no more than one to three months. As president of the business unit, it would have been at least five to ten years. Had he ever made it to CEO, it would have been fifteen to twenty years.

Part of the difficulty in making this shift is that the move into organizational leadership is less clearly defined than is the move into operational leadership. The transition into a first workplace leadership role is often sudden and sometimes brutal—but it's never mistakable. You suddenly become responsible for not just your own work but also the work of those in your care; that responsibility is often compounded by the fact that you find yourself leading people you were just working with as peers. The shift into organizational leadership is typically more gradual; and, because it's gradual, it's easier to miss the changing focus that's occurring.

THE SPECIFIC SKILLS AND BEHAVIORS OF THE THREE DIMENSIONS

So what are the different functions and responses? The distinction between organizational leadership, operational leadership, and people leadership is easy to acknowledge intuitively. But what skills and behaviors characterize each one? What functions does each one fulfill? Once you have an understanding of their key functions, it's easy to grasp the nature of Mike's demise.

Organizational leadership is characterized by three fundamental functions, which form the acronym CAS:

> ### ORGANIZATIONAL LEADERSHIP
>
> **C** – Creating and clarifying the direction
> **A** – Aligning the organization and resources to that direction
> **S** – Selling and promoting the message of the direction

Organizational leadership's first focus is external; its primary concern is the organization's long-term relevance and contribution. It therefore clarifies and establishes the organization's direction (its purpose and vision) and the qualitative means of getting there (its values). Its internal focus is therefore directed less to the organization's day-to-day operations and more to the organization's alignment to its direction, making sure that the components of the organization are in step. To do so, the organization needs to sell and promote the message of that direction in such a way that everyone embraces both its purpose and vision and its values in the pursuit of that direction.

That's the kind of leadership Mike's staff and corporate bosses wanted and expected. It wasn't what Mike provided.

Instead, he provided excellent operational leadership—inappropriately, since he was usurping the role of his operational leaders. The functions of operational leadership form the acronym POM:

> ### OPERATIONAL LEADERSHIP
>
> **P** – Planning and shaping processes
> **O** – Organizing and controlling
> **M** – Measuring and problem solving

With a focus on execution and operational excellence, operational leadership takes the direction set by organizational leadership and figures out the most effective way of pursuing that direction, and it does so by planning and shaping the way the work is done, by organizing and controlling the work, and by measuring results and solving problems of execution.

The relationship between organizational leadership and operational leadership has always been uneasy, and Mike's experience is all too common. The tension between the two has been well documented by thinkers such as John Kotter, Warren Bennis, and many others. For the most part, the tension has been framed in terms of *leadership* (referred to here as *organizational leadership*) as opposed to *management* (referred to here as *operational leadership*). The tension is clearly very real; both are critical when appropriately applied, and the absence of either has a profoundly negative impact on the organization.

The third leadership dimension is people leadership, and for Mike to do this well, he needed to master the following three key functions, which form the acronym SEM:

PEOPLE LEADERSHIP

S – Selecting and matching the right people
E – Explaining and clarifying expectations
M – Motivating and developing

The focus of people leadership is on bringing out the best in the people you lead, whatever your level of leadership. Whether you are a frontline manager or the CEO or a business unit leader, you need to be strong in selecting and matching the right people for the job, you need to make sure that expectations of them are clear, you need to know how to motivate your people, and you need to be committed to developing them.

HOW PEOPLE LEADERSHIP FITS IN

How did Mike fare in terms of people leadership? Not as well as you might think. Even though he had solid people skills, was fundamentally a likable person, and knew how to get along with people, those skills didn't automatically translate into effective people leadership. Being likable, even charismatic, is quite different from having an intentional commitment to bringing out the best in people. If anything, Mike's likability was a handicap, because he mistook people's responsiveness to his personality as responsiveness to his leadership skills.

Mike showed little evidence of the skills associated with people leadership. His hires and promotions were haphazard. He didn't give much thought to the real strengths of his direct reports and how to match their knowledge, skills, and talent to the contexts that most needed them. He hired mostly on gut feelings, and he struck out more often than he connected. He did a poor job of explaining his expectations, and for the most part he lived under the assumption that his expectations were as clear to everyone else as they were to him. In Mike's mind, motivating meant delivering a high-energy pep talk (which he did well). Developing his people was reduced to making public programs open to anyone who wanted to go to them. There was nothing intentional, planned, or purposeful in the development of his staff.

So Mike's problems were twofold. Not only did he miss the changing mix of organizational leadership and operational leadership, he also misunderstood the real nature of people leadership.

From a research-validation perspective, the focus on people leadership skills is relatively recent. Pieces of it have been the subject of research for some time (as far back as the 1960s, for example, with Frederick Herzberg on motivation), but few have conducted broader research. Back in the early 1980s, I came across some research by the University of Tel Aviv, which wanted to find out what motivates good combat performance. In battle, a soldier can run, hide, panic, shoot the enemy, or shoot fellow soldiers. . . . So what makes a soldier perform well under fire? The study was conducted during the Arab-Israeli wars, and the researchers expected to uncover motivations such as national defense and patriotism. They came to a different and surprising finding: the one overarching factor was the soldier's relationship with his commanding officer. If it was a good relationship, combat performance was high. If it was poor, combat performance was low.

Precious little research on a larger scale was done on the subject in subsequent years until Gallup took up the theme in the late 1990s and applied it to more than eighty thousand managers in more than four hundred companies (described in Buckingham and Coffman's *First, Break All the Rules*). Their question was Why are some organizations better than others at retaining good people (good people, not average people)? Their conclusions paralleled the Tel Aviv research: managers trump organizations. A company may have a very attractive benefits package and beautiful surroundings with every possible amenity, but that focus misses the point. Such assets can recruit good people, but they don't keep them. What keeps them is the relationship the new employees develop with their managers. Managers *always* trump organizations. The Tel Aviv and Gallup research underscored the fact that the managers who keep the good people are those who are strong in the skills captured in the SEM functions.

THE THREE DIMENSIONS AND THE LEADERSHIP CUBE

What would have helped Mike? He would certainly have been helped if he had understood the concept of the three dimensions of leadership, and he would have been well served if he had understood the CAS, POM, and SEM functions.

That still would not have been quite enough. He needed to understand how the functions interact at any given level of leadership; he needed a framework to understand how to apply the three dimensions appropriately with each promotion. He needed to understand the Leadership Cube shown in Figure 27.

The Leadership Cube is a tool that provides the framework to understand the relationship among the three dimensions; it allows you to figure out what great leadership looks like at whatever level of leadership you find yourself.

The face of the cube shows the relationship between organizational leadership and operational leadership (see Figure 25). The rest of the cube represents the relationship of people leadership to organizational and operational leadership.

The Leadership Cube captures three important principles for competent leadership—principles that will help spell out where Mike's leadership competence broke down.

The Impact of People Leadership

> *The first principle:* If people leadership is absent, *organizational leadership and operational leadership will be less effective.*

Well-implemented organizational leadership (CAS) and operational leadership (POM) without solid people leadership (SEM) is a flimsy edifice, almost two-dimensional. It will be easily toppled. The stability of competent leadership comes from the right mix of organizational leadership and operational leadership with strong selection, clear expectations, relevant motivation, and intentional development. With a strong commitment to people leadership, leadership within an organization can become genuinely three-dimensional; without this commitment, leadership remains flat and incomplete (see Figure 28). The difference in both organizational and individual performance is profound.

FIGURE 27. THREE COMPONENTS OF LEADERSHIP: THE LEADERSHIP CUBE

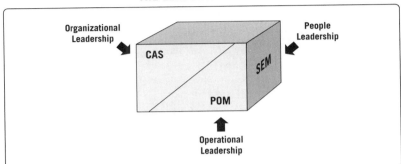

FIGURE 28. CONTRASTING STRONG AND WEAK PEOPLE LEADERSHIP

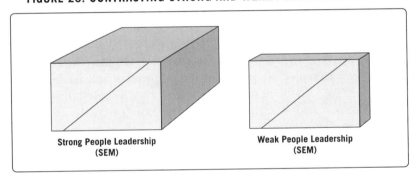

Strong People Leadership (SEM)

Weak People Leadership (SEM)

The stronger the people leadership, the stronger the organization: the more firmly in place the critical functions of people leadership, the more effectively the distinctions between organizational leadership and operational leadership can be taught and implemented. A solid commitment to developing the people leadership skills in the organization strengthens the exercise of operational and organizational leadership skills.

The Application of People Leadership

The second principle: People leadership will be less *effective if it is not intentionally applied at every level of leadership.*

FIGURE 29. APPLYING THE RIGHT LEADERSHIP MIX AT EACH LEVEL OF LEADERSHIP

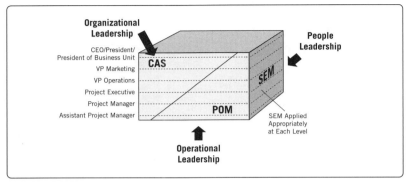

People leadership doesn't happen without a great deal of intentionality, and intentionality can only prosper when the environment encourages it. In one sense, the blame for Mike's demise can be laid unhesitatingly at the feet of the organization, because the company had never fostered an environment that allowed people leadership to flourish. Mike had never been taught how to select well, how to lay out his expectations without ambiguity, how to create and focus motivation—and, most injurious of all, no one had modeled investment in Mike's development so that he could turn around and invest in the development of his people.

Practicing the habits and skills of people leadership was as alien to him as president of the business unit as it had been as assistant project manager, but that deficiency was much more costly at the top of the cube. Some of his misjudgments involved poor selections: the finance director he hired didn't work out, his promotion of a senior account manager to sales manager was misguided, and, without the right kind of development, neither had a chance. If Mike had learned and developed people leadership habits early on, he would have been applying them as president with comfort and skill. Not only that—he would have been making sure that everyone in his organization was applying them appropriately at every level. The dotted lines in Figure 29 represent where people leadership should have been applied at each level of the organizational–operational leadership mix. But that never happened. In Mike's case and under his leadership, those dotted lines just weren't there.

**FIGURE 30. STRONG PEOPLE LEADERSHIP:
WEAK ORGANIZATIONAL-OPERATIONAL LEADERSHIP**

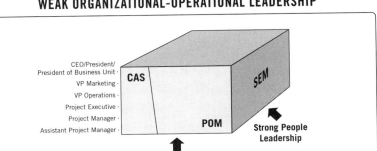

The Right Mix

> *The third principle: People leadership will be most
> effective when the right mix exists between organiza-
> tional and operational leadership at every level of
> leadership.*

Organizational leadership and operational leadership need people
leadership to give strength to their implementation; people leadership
needs organizational leadership and operational leadership to give it
context.

People are best developed when organizational leadership creates
and clarifies a compelling sense of direction, when the organization
and its resources are intentionally aligned to that direction, when the
message is clearly articulated and promoted (the CAS functions), and
when operational leadership is efficiently supporting and executing
that direction (the POM functions). When the mix is healthy, people
leadership can flourish, because it will be appropriately applied.

If people leadership is strong and the mix of the other two is
weak, people will be intentionally selected, but for the wrong kind of
function. Expectations will be clarified, but they'll be the wrong
expectations. People will be motivated and developed, but in the
wrong direction. People will perform well, but not necessarily in the
organization's interests, because those interests will not have been
clearly articulated by the organizational leaders. The cube will look
like the one in Figure 30.

FIGURE 31. MIKE'S LEADERSHIP CUBE

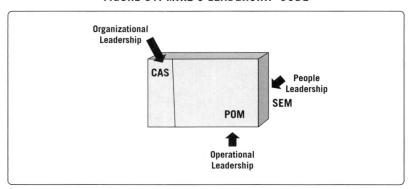

THE REST OF THE STORY

It should be evident by now that Mike's leadership mix was anything but healthy. He had the organizational–operational leadership mix all wrong, and his people leadership was flimsy (see Figure 31). It wouldn't take much to topple his cube—and in the end it didn't.

Mike did get fired. It was painful, but, by the time it came, it was widely seen as inevitable.

He took a six-month sabbatical, an enforced one, admittedly—but he was determined to figure out what had gone wrong. He even took the risky move of turning down a reasonably attractive offer soon after his departure. He figured that financially he could survive the break, and he didn't want to go back to a leadership role so soon without knowing how to do it differently.

Mike became a student of leadership. He also became a student of himself, as he uncovered and his strengths and weaknesses and also his aspirations. He wondered if he would be best suited to an operational leadership role and should focus his efforts on finding that type of position. But, as he became familiar with the three dimensions of leadership, he felt drawn to organizational leadership—now that he understood what it required.

Mike had some good things going for him. His integrity was an asset, and he hadn't muddied the waters with unethical or immoral conduct. He knew his issues had to do with competence, not character. In the character–competence grid in Figure 32 (introduced in Chapter 3), he was clearly in the high character–low competence

FIGURE 32. CHARACTER AND COMPETENCE IN LEADERSHIP

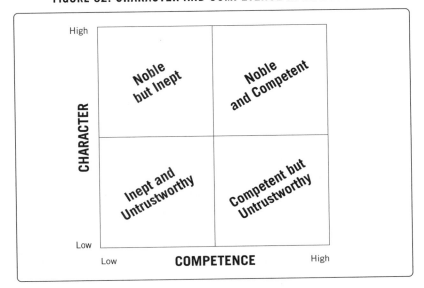

quadrant, but he felt that by learning the skills he'd been missing, he had a good chance of moving into the high character–high competence quadrant. Great leadership was not beyond his grasp.

And, he concluded wryly, if it didn't work out, he could always teach or be a consultant.

In the end, he was offered a position that gave him the opportunity to implement what he'd been learning. Mike did become a teacher in a sense—he taught those he was leading to apply the principles of the cube to their own levels of leadership and to teach others to do the same. Over time, Mike became appreciated for what he had always wanted—for his competence as a leader.

For every Mike, there are many who come to grief but don't attempt the same learning and self-analysis that Mike embarked on. But the lesson from Mike is this: it's never too late to learn. If you are in your twenties or early thirties, learning these principles will give you a better framework to handle and negotiate the midcareer challenges and course corrections that will inevitably unfold. If you are in midcareer, these principles will give you the framework to learn what course corrections you need to make; and, if you are in the last stretches, these principles will help you shape your legacy.

Let the principles of the Leadership Cube become an ally in your personal growth as a leader and in the growth of your organization. Allow them to provide you with the framework to create a practice of leadership that is genuinely complete because it is genuinely three-dimensional. Use them to help you think deeply and differently, about your leadership practices and about how leadership is practiced in your organization. Let them be your measuring stick for the practice of highly competent leadership.

The next chapter is about the organization: understanding how it works is a necessary condition for exploring the qualities of organizational, operational, and people leadership in greater depth. As these three dimensions become part of your leadership capabilities, you'll be able to practice the kind of leadership your circumstances require —and, most important, you'll be making sure everyone else is exercising the kind of leadership their role requires.

Yours will not only be a well-run ship with a clear sense of direction—it will be a ship people will work on with pride and enthusiasm.

7

THE MYSTERY OF ORGANIZATIONS

Understanding How Your Organization Works— and How to Shape It

Michelangelo was once asked what he saw in a rough, uncut block of marble. "An angel," he replied, "imprisoned in the marble, and I must carve until I set him free." Up to now, the focus has been on the artist—the leader. This chapter focuses on the block of marble—the organization.

When people try to explain how organizations work, they typically use metaphors—an army at war, a machine in motion, an organism in nature, and so on. This chapter looks at organizations using three different metaphors:

- *A journey:* Organizations are vehicles created to reach a destination, and, from the moment of their launch, every day adds a new page to the story of their odyssey. Great leaders guide that odyssey.

- *A life span:* Organizations are born, they grow, they age, and eventually they die. Great leaders understand these cycles; they know when to consolidate and when to reenergize. Most of all, they know how to beat the aging process.

■ *A tribe:* Organizations have a common interest and an agreed-on way of doing things. They have a recognizable culture. Great leaders shape that culture.

Each image reveals something different; together they tell a great deal. They lay the foundation for a better understanding of the three dimensions of leadership—organizational leadership, operational leadership, and people leadership—by providing the context in which the three are exercised.

ORGANIZATIONS AS VEHICLES ON A JOURNEY

"It's been a grand journey," Winston Churchill said near the end of his life, "well worth making once." Life as a journey is a theme we understand well, and most of us have encountered the likes of Mark Twain's *Huckleberry Finn.* If your English teacher was more adventurous, you may have been exposed to Homer's *Odyssey,* Bunyan's *Pilgrim's Progress,* Chaucer's *Canterbury Tales,* or even Dante's *Divine Comedy,* which begins, "Midway on our life's journey, I found myself in a dark wood."

If that phase of your existence is an educational blur, consider some of the movies you've watched—*The Wizard of Oz,* the *Back to the Future* movies, *Apollo 13, Saving Private Ryan, Master and Commander, Titanic, Gladiator, Lord of the Rings,* and countless others. All tell the story of people on a journey.

Organizations can be thought of as people on a journey: when someone new joins, you "welcome them aboard." When you leave, you tell people you "had quite a ride," maybe "a rough ride." Karl Albrecht compared the organization to a northbound train and Jim Collins to a bus. Whatever the metaphoric means of transport, organizations are on a journey, and like a vehicle without a destination, an organization without direction doesn't make sense—which may explain why many organizations don't make sense; they have no clear destination.

An organization needs a destination. It needs a point on the horizon to head toward. We call that *vision.* It also needs a clear sense of why it started the journey and why it's on a particular road. We call that *purpose,* or *mission.* It also needs a clear set of principles to guide its behaviors as it travels. We call those *values.*

FIGURE 33. THE ORGANIZATION ON A JOURNEY

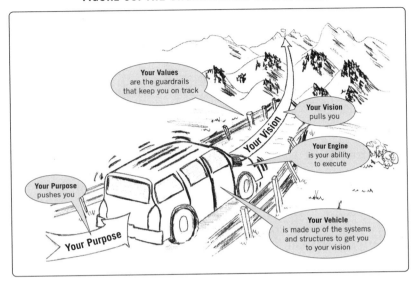

Your purpose—the reason you got on this road is what pushes you. Your vision—that point on the horizon you strive toward—is your destination. And your values—the guardrails—keep you on track (see Figure 33).

The vehicle is your organization. It needs to be the right kind of vehicle to get you there, appropriate for the terrain you're covering, and suited to your purpose and vision. The vehicle is powered by executing your strategies—the engine that keeps it moving.

The success of the journey is in the hands of the leadership, where all three dimensions of leadership function well (see Table 1).

Organizational leadership takes ownership of developing and defining the purpose, vision, and values. That is, it clarifies why the vehicle is on the road it's on (purpose or mission), identifies the point to head for (vision), and makes sure behavioral barriers keep it from veering off course (values). It also makes sure the organization and its resources are aligned to that purpose, vision, and values. If the vehicle is inappropriate, organizational leadership reconfigures its design and structure. And finally, it sells the direction—creating a shared purpose, vision, and values—communicating endlessly, listening patiently, explaining creatively, honoring input, adjusting appropriately, and distributing ownership.

TABLE 1. THE THREE DIMENSIONS OF LEADERSHIP

Organizational Leadership (CAS)	Operational Leadership (POM)	People Leadership (SEM)
■ **C**reating and clarifying the direction ■ **A**ligning the organization and its resources to that direction ■ **S**elling and promoting the message of the direction	■ **P**lanning and shaping processes ■ **O**rganizing and controlling ■ **M**easuring and problem solving	■ **S**electing and matching the right people ■ **E**xplaining and clarifying expectations ■ **M**otivating and developing

If organizational leadership is properly exercised, *operational leadership* can be fully exercised: making sure the vehicle runs smoothly. Operational leadership maintains the engine that provides the energy for the organization's forward momentum, and it makes sure that all parts of the vehicle function well together. When something goes wrong, it has a process in place for solving the problem and getting back on the road.

People leadership focuses on the people inside the vehicle. It's one thing to have a clear purpose and destination, it's another thing to have a well-functioning vehicle to get there in, and it's yet another thing to have people in the vehicle who know what they're doing. Without the right people, the vehicle may not move at all.

Such is the stuff of well-led organizations. The three dimensions come together in the Leadership Cube (see Chapter 6; shown again in Figure 34). With this kind of leadership, there's hardly a journey your organization can't undertake.

ORGANIZATIONS AS A LIFE SPAN

Although all journeys come to an end, some end before the final destination is reached. Over time, the journey gets harder, and the organization begins to feel its age. Organizations are dynamic, living organisms: they are born, they grow, they grow old, and eventually they die. There's nothing static about organizations, which makes them such a challenge to lead. They go through discernible stages, or life cycles (see Figure 35).

FIGURE 34. THE JOURNEY'S LEADERSHIP CUBE

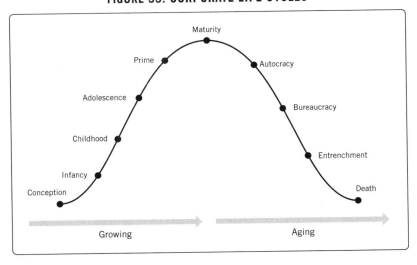

Organizational Leadership:
Makes sure the vehicle
is on the right road,
heading for the right
destination, and
appropriately equipped
to get there

CAS

SEM

POM

People Leadership:
Makes sure the people
in the vehicle are
well suited, well trained,
and well resourced
for the roles they fill

Operational Leadership:
Makes sure the vehicle is
functioning well and capable
of reaching its destination

FIGURE 35. CORPORATE LIFE CYCLES

Maturity

Prime

Autocracy

Adolescence

Bureaucracy

Childhood

Entrenchment

Infancy

Conception

Death

Growing

Aging

The starting point of every organization is a concept in the mind of the founder or founders. Many are stillborn or die in infancy. Those that survive need virtually constant care at first, and the survival rate still isn't high. But, in time, the energy put into nurture begins to pay off, and the organization demonstrates the often constant, exhausting, and spontaneous energy of a child. Physical growth is often dramatic, and now the organization finds itself in the adolescent tension between a mature, powerful body and an immature, inexperienced mind. Successful negotiation of its adolescence propels the organization into its prime; the organization will never look better or more appealing.

Typically, at maturity, a subtle shift takes place. The organization looks so good that its leaders become more concerned with preserving than with creating. The organization, as it ages, develops bureaucratic structures designed to solidify its very real gains and its culture is overtaken by an autocratic style that pushes it toward entrenchment, senility, and, ultimately, death. The time frames for these cycles can be very short or very long; an organization can get to prime in one year or even bureaucracy in six months. It can get stuck in adolescence for years. It can completely bypass prime and maturity. It's not primarily an issue of time.

This process has an inevitability to it that few leaders recognize. More accurately, it's inevitable if inadequate attention is given to the tension that exists at the top of the curve—the tension between maintaining a healthy, flexible opportunism as the market changes and the ability to realign the organization to these new opportunities.

The task of organizational leaders is to create and clarify the direction—or re-create and reclarify that direction as markets change or goals are accomplished and visions fulfilled. There comes a point when it's the vision beyond the vision that matters. Kennedy's goal for NASA in 1961 was bold, daring, and compelling: landing a man on the moon by the end of the decade. The problem was that when NASA achieved it—a remarkable achievement—they had nothing to follow; there was no re-creation and reclarification of its direction. The research Collins and Porras did for *Built to Last* bears this out: companies that were built to last found a way of re-creating a direction and a vision, often with bold and compelling aspirations that brought new life and energy to the whole organization. At risky times in their existence, IBM bet on the new computer called the IBM 360 (up to that point, the largest privately funded project ever undertaken), and Boeing bet the entire resources of the company on the 707 (and again later on the 747)—both gutsy moves that pulled the companies back to their prime and spared them from slipping into autocracy (see Figure 36).

The strength of prime is in its entrepreneurial mind-set; the strength of maturity is in its ability to align the organization around its entrepreneurial drives. As the alignment becomes established, leaders are tempted to solidify that alignment. If they do, the organization

FIGURE 36. RECYCLING THE CORPORATE LIFE CYCLE

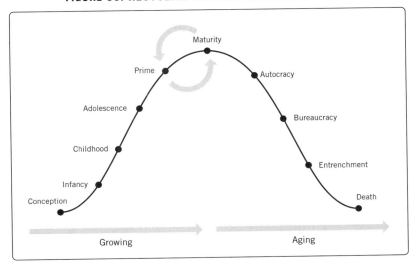

starts drifting downward toward autocracy. If, instead, they reinvigorate its entrepreneurial drives, the organization moves back to prime and sustains its energy and growth.

The challenge of leadership is getting to prime and, once there, staying there. On the way up, the leadership challenges are fairly immediate and short-term—especially in conception, infancy, and childhood, where the chief need is survival. With every step up the curve, the need for clarifying the organization's direction—not just its vision and purpose, but also its values—becomes more acute, and getting to prime is impossible without creating and clarifying direction.

Once at the top of the curve, the challenge is maintaining the tension between relevant direction and corresponding alignment—two key functions of organizational leadership. For organizations on the downward curve, it's the same challenge; it's just a whole lot harder to pull off in the face of an autocratic, bureaucratic mind-set. It's been done; Lou Gerstner did it with IBM, but it's rare. For organizations on the upward curve, the challenge is different: while the need for clarity around direction is still critical, short-term survival needs can legitimately preempt the sustained preoccupation with long-term aspirations.

Corporate life-cycle theory is a relatively recent field of research. Its best exponent is Ichak Adizes, who calls the stages Courtship,

Infancy, Go-Go, Adolescence, Prime, Stable, Aristocracy, Early Bureaucracy, Bureaucracy, and Death. His message is addressed primarily to organizational leaders, whose focus is external relevance (and whose functions are creating and clarifying direction, aligning the organization to that direction, and selling that direction), and secondarily to operational leadership, whose focus is internal efficiency (and whose functions are process planning, organizing and controlling, and measuring and problem solving). He identifies four distinct leadership functions—Performance, Administration, Entrepreneurship, and Integration—each of which plays differently at different points on the life-cycle curve. He provides an elaborate combination with different weightings for each point on the curve, but, in its simplest form, two have to do with the short term and two with the long term:

- *Performance* focuses on what the client wants now (offers short-term effectiveness).

- *Administration* runs a tight ship (provides short-term efficiency).

- *Entrepreneurship* innovates (sees tomorrow's need for the client and knows what to do today to satisfy it, offering long-term effectiveness).

- *Integration* aligns the organization around the innovation designed to satisfy the client's future needs (builds for long-term efficiency).

So what does this mean to you as a leader? A great deal. Where you are—or where your organization is—on the life-cycle curve makes a difference in how you lead. The great value of corporate life cycles is giving us a picture of prime, the stages in getting there, and the pitfalls of passing through it. If you are in the earlier stages of your organization's evolution, focus more on the short term; long-term planning without attention to short-term success is a recipe for premature death. But, once you get through short-term imperatives, it won't be long before the increasing pressures of growth will bring the need to clarify the purpose, vision, and values of the organization so that behavior is driven not by personalities but by a clear purpose, a strong vision, and a unifying set of values.

If you are at the top of the curve, your challenge will be the juggling act of flexibly aligning and realigning the organization to a fresh, live, and relevant vision that keeps the organization energized and engaged.

And, if you are on the downward side of the curve . . . you have a challenge! Not an insurmountable one, but a tough one nonetheless, because you'll need to change the culture.

ORGANIZATIONS AS A TRIBE

Colin Turnbull, an Oxford-educated anthropologist, focused mostly on African pigmy tribes. As part of his research, he spent a year with a tribe living deep in an equatorial forest. No one from the tribe had ever ventured outside the forest; but, by the end of the year, he persuaded one of the pigmies to come out of the forest with him. When they cleared the forest, they were met with a vast panoramic view of the savannah—huge open spaces, sparse trees, rock formations, distant mountains, and people and animals moving around some distance away. As the pigmy slowly absorbed the scene, he reached out his hand to grab the figures in the distance.

His problem was one of perspective. He had never been in an environment where he had to focus farther than twenty feet, and now he was faced with a panorama measured not in feet but in miles. His underdeveloped sense of perspective suddenly became a huge handicap.

Perspective is a function of culture. Every organization has a unique culture, and that culture defines how people inside look at the world outside. When they step outside into unfamiliar territory, they do strange things—like reaching out to grab figures in the distance. That's why every new job with a new organization is an exercise in culture shock.

"The unique and essential function of leadership," Edgar Schein tells us, "is the manipulation of culture." Now that culture has been recognized as the unseen force that shapes the way things get done, it's no wonder that leaders are looking for resources to shape it. "I came to see, in my time at IBM," Lou Gerstner writes, "that culture isn't just one aspect of the game—it is the game."

In leadership, then, the intangibles are paramount. As Gerstner pointed out, "The really important rules aren't written down anywhere." It's what you don't see or aren't trained to see that blindsides you. This is counterintuitive, because leaders instinctively look to the tangibles—the quantifiable, measurable, visible, and verifiable data, systems, and structures. They use financial and operational data to shape their decisions and they create organizational charts to implement them; when the data produce unsatisfactory results, they work harder on the data.

The real drivers, however, are elsewhere. The drivers that shape the data and define their quality are the underlying attitudes, the deeply embedded values, the unspoken belief systems, the unconscious habits, the unwritten rules of success, the unchallenged assumptions, and the ingrained patterns of communication—not the kind of thing they teach you in business school. The tangible and concrete data essential to the organization's leaders are processed through this mill of invisible forces that more than anything else determine the quality and nature of the data, systems, and structures they rely on. Leaders can read the spreadsheets and analyze the data, they can change the names and titles inside the boxes, but it's the fuzzy yet critical intangibles that leaders need to grasp and shape. When Edgar Schein talks about "the manipulation of culture," he is talking about the leader's ability to manage these intangible and unseen forces.

The question is How do you identify these intangible forces? How do you shape a culture? How do you transform an organization? Consolidating and aligning the organization's beliefs and values is a daunting task. You need a framework to mold and shape the intangibles.

THE SEVEN ELEMENTS OF AN ORGANIZATION

Every organization is composed of seven basic elements. Everything the organization does, everything it attempts, every decision it makes, and every facet of its personality is tied to these basic elements. Whatever its industry or sector, whatever its legal structure, whatever its tax status, whatever its ownership, and whatever its size, these elements represent the sum of the organization. If you understand these elements and how they interconnect, you understand organizations—your own or any other.

These are the first six basic elements:

■ *Leadership:* The organization's capacity to provide leadership on all three dimensions (organizational leadership, operational leadership, and people leadership).

- *Purpose and values:* The sense of clarity in the organization's purpose and values.

- *Vision:* The organization's capacity to not only set direction but think strategically.

- *Systems and structures:* The organization's ability to align the systems and structures to support and further the purpose, values, and vision.

- *People selection, development, and succession:* The organization's ability to align its selection, development, and succession processes to the organization's purpose, values, and vision.

- *Execution:* The structure and process in place to make sure that the organization's purpose, values, and vision are translated into goals it can work on.

These six shape the seventh:

- *Culture:* The personality of the organization and its impact, positive or negative, on the accomplishment of the organization's goals.

None of these is likely to be new to you, and some of them you may have already given some thought to. But just as important as understanding each one is understanding how they connect with each other. Unlike loose atoms bouncing off each other, they have a definite interconnectedness; and, while all are important, not all have equal weight all the time. Effective leadership is knowing how to address each one appropriately and systematically, using it as needed to align the culture to the organization's purpose, vision, and values. Master these elements and you master organizational transformation and realignment.

Integrating the Seven Elements

When leaders understand how these elements integrate with each other and how they influence each other, they can better assess the organization's strengths and weaknesses and, thus, intentionally and systematically engineer the realignment and transformation their organizations need. Instead of reacting and responding to issues as they emerge, these leaders frame behavior from a sharpened set of priorities and avoid the temptation of unthinking action on one hand and inactive thinking on the other.

FIGURE 37. KEY ELEMENTS OF AN ORGANIZATION

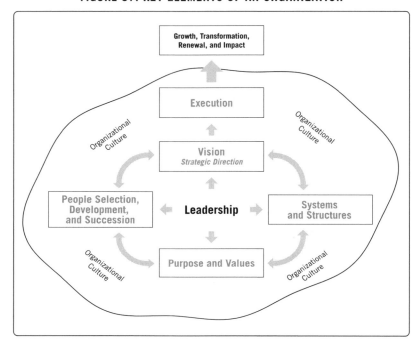

Figure 37 describes the relationships between the seven elements; what follows is a brief description of each. Each is amplified in the following chapters as they are addressed by the appropriate leadership function.

The squiggly perimeter defines the culture of the organization. It is not easily identifiable, easily recognizable, or easily defined. It's malleable; it moves and changes shape in response to forces inside and outside it. The stronger the organization's culture, the less the external impact, but no culture is impervious to the external environment pushing against it, sometimes seeping through, sometimes breaking through, its boundaries.

Your culture is the character of the organization. It's the soul and personality of your organization, and just as no two individuals have the same personality, so no two organizations have the same personality. Almost every adjective that can be attributed to an individual can be attributed to an organization. Organizations can be exciting, lively, and adventuresome, and they can be dour, dull, and boring. They can be warm and friendly, and they can be cold and impersonal. They can be disciplined and organized or spontaneous and disorganized.

Like human personality and behavioral styles, organizational cultures can be measured and defined. To measure one, you look for the way the intangibles are expressed. How, for example, is status allocated? How is authority perceived? What gets rewarded? How is success defined? How do people communicate? How is conflict handled? How are relationships viewed? How is learning engaged? Who are the heroes? How is time viewed? What are the traditions, the rites, and the rituals?

Some researchers have translated these questions into measurement models. In *Corporate cultures* (1982), Terrence Deal and Allan Kennedy offered a typology using feedback and risk-taking to define four cultures: the tough-guy macho culture, the work hard and play hard culture, the bet-your-company culture, and the process culture. Later, Terrence Deal teamed up with Lee Bolman on *Reframing Organizations* (1997) to offer four "frames": the structural frame, the human resource frame, the political frame, and the symbolic frame. In *The Character of the Corporation* (1998), Rob Goffee and Gareth Jones offered four perspectives based on the level of solidarity and sociability that exists within an organization: the networked culture, the mercenary culture, the fragmented culture, and the communal culture. Charles Handy jumped in with *The Gods of Management* (1995), offering a typology based on four Greek gods: Zeus, Apollo, Dionysus, and Athena. Edgar Schein focused on the mechanisms of uncovering corporate cultures, whatever the nomenclature ascribed to them.

For all the value of clarifying your culture, that is not what you focus on. You need to know what kind of culture you have—but your interest is in shaping your culture, engineering a profound transformation of the very soul of your organization. Your culture is like a thermometer: it tells you the temperature. More useful is the thermostat, and the items below are the dials on your thermostat.

Leadership. Engineering cultural transformation is a leadership function. Cultures seldom change by themselves—at least, not for the good. Leaders are the greatest influence on the way the organization is shaped, transformed, and renewed. They touch, shape, and influence all the other elements: purpose and values; vision; systems and structures; people selection, development and succession; and execution. Their role is pivotal.

Purpose, values, and vision. Great organizations are led by leaders who think ten, twenty, even thirty years into the future, not just in terms of leadership but also in terms of what the organization will look like. Effective leaders start by focusing on the why (the organization's purpose), the how (in terms of its values), and the what (its vision). Once these are clear, the leadership can focus on the how in terms of systems and structures and people selection, development, and succession. Clearly articulated purpose, values, and vision make it much easier to align selection and development, as well as succession planning, those elements: it's much easier to hire people who embrace them, to train people to live by them, and to identify leaders who will support them. And when the final how, in terms of execution, is consistent with the rest of the elements, the organization takes on an unbeatable dynamic energy. The final result is growth, change, and impact.

But it doesn't always work that way. If leaders inadequately define and articulate the organization's purpose, values, and vision, they will have nothing to align to. Their systems and structures and their people selection and development strategies will be at cross-purposes, and execution will be weak and haphazard, leaving a weak and dysfunctional culture. So great leaders focus on the core—on the deeply held beliefs within the organization. They encode them in a clear purpose, with well-defined values.

It's one thing to create a sense of vision; it's another to create a sense of shared vision. Great leaders thus focus not only on the clarity of purpose, vision, and values but also on the level of buy-in to purpose, vision, and values. If there's little clarity and little buy-in (see Figure 38), leaders will need to work on clarity before they work on buy-in.

The order, by the way, is interchangeable—purpose-values-vision or purpose-vision-values—which is why I refer to them interchangeably throughout these chapters. They come as a package and all three are necessary and interrelated.

Systems and structures. With purpose, values, and vision in place, the right systems and structures to support and further them are needed. In its simplest expression, an organization exists to make decisions and to reward the execution of those decisions (or punish their nonexecution), and, to do so, the organization develops systems and

FIGURE 38. TWO KEY INGREDIENTS

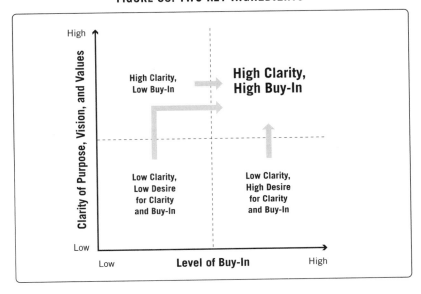

structures that support the decision-making process and the reward structures. It doesn't take long for the systems and structures to take on a life of their own, and they can end up becoming counterproductive, working against the direction the leaders want to take the organization. As Don Berwick, CEO of the Institute for Healthcare Improvement, has wryly commented, "Every system is perfectly designed to produce the results you're already getting." So good leaders assess their decision-making processes as well as their reward structures, and they identify the ones they need and the ones they don't.

Structures are easier to address than systems. It's easy to draw organization charts with boxes and lines, but it's hard to think about what actually happens between the boxes. And systems are pervasive: every unit in your organization has its own systems, and every unit is part of the larger system of the entire organization, and the organization itself is part of a still larger system of economic and market forces. These interdependencies may be unseen or unacknowledged. Great leaders, however, understand systems thinking. They uncover the links and interdependencies within the organization and direct them so that the systems support and reinforce the organization's purpose, values, and vision. (More on this in Chapter 9.)

People selection, development, and succession. Every organization acknowledges the importance of developing people. For some, it's genuine, and for others, it's lip service to a now widely accepted business axiom. Less common is the deliberate and intentional aligning of selection and development strategies to the purpose, values, and vision of the organization.

With the first four elements clearly identified and applied, selection, development, and succession issues take on a new look. You align selection and development strategies to your values and strategic direction. When your purpose, vision, and values are clear, you will look for and hire people who share your values, reducing the costly consequences of mistaken hires.

The benefits don't stop at selection. With a clear sense of purpose, vision, and values, your development strategies become more intentional and purposeful. You look for ways to match talent to the organization's direction, and you develop your people's ability to function in line with your organization's critical success factors. More than that, you develop people not only for the present needs of the organization, but also for its future needs. In other words, you deliberately and systematically implement succession thinking and succession planning, for specific jobs and also for the generational transfer of the organization to its future leaders.

The larger the organization, the greater the likelihood of inconsistent selection, development, and succession strategies. It is not unusual for one site to have several training and development initiatives being pursued concurrently. Without a clear framework shaped by the organization's purpose, values, and vision, the selection, development, and succession strategies will be incoherent and inconsistent.

Execution. Execution is the element most leaders turn to first. Organizations, after all, are designed to produce results, and, without execution, you don't get results. But when leaders focus on execution outside the framework of a clear purpose, values, and vision, they create a highly dysfunctional culture. They set goals, but those goals have no meaningful context, and will ultimately pull the organization in different, even conflicting, directions.

The challenge of execution is to keep short- and long-term goals meaningfully and intimately connected to the organization's everyday purpose, vision, and values. Organizations often succumb to the demands of the present because the future they want and the present they live in seem utterly disconnected. Leaders end up either discarding the whole notion of purpose and vision or maintaining and promoting a purpose and vision at the cost of a serious credibility gap between the stated vision and the daily reality. They end up pursuing short-term goals or developing inconsistent long-term goals.

The challenge of execution is best met by identifying the elements that are absolutely essential to the purpose and vision—the *critical success factors*—which then become the framework for defining everything everyone does and every goal being pursued at any given time. (More on this in Chapter 9.)

When an Element Is Missing or Ignored

Ignoring or missing any one of the elements that make up the organization has significant implications. When leaders address all the elements, their efforts at transformation and renewal have a real likelihood of success; but when one is missed or ignored, the leaders' aspirations for reshaping the culture will be compromised.

Figure 39 suggests what might happen if an element is missing. Levels one to six reflect the absence of a different element at each level. Each level assumes (somewhat unrealistically) that all other elements are in place. In reality, more than one element is typically missing, multiplying the impact on the quality of those that remain. Level seven, highlighted, is the ideal where all elements are functioning well.

The most critical abscence is at level one—the absence of clear leadership. If leadership is unclear or leadership capacity is weak, there is little chance of the organization's purpose, vision, and values being well defined and articulated. With poor definition and articulation of purpose, values, and vision, people will be selected and developed without reference to the organization's direction, systems and structures will not be aligned, and execution will be disjointed and haphazard—because of the absence of the intentional application of the three dimensions of leadership, each applying its focus to the appropriate element (see Figure 40). Leaders are indeed an organization's greatest asset.

Organizations are multifaceted. Vehicles on a journey, organisms growing and aging, and tribes adjusting to the savannah—these

FIGURE 39. THE CHANGE EQUATION: WHAT HAPPENS WHEN ONE ELEMENT IS MISSING OR IGNORED?

Level	Leadership Capacity	Purpose and Values	Vision	Systems and Structures	Selection, Development, and Succession	Execution	= Result
7	Leadership Capacity	+ Purpose and Values	+ Vision	+ Systems and Structures	+ Selection, Development, and Succession	+ Execution	= Healthy growth and impact; successful realignment; dynamic transformation
6	Leadership Capacity	+ Purpose and Values	+ Vision	+ Systems and Structures	+ Selection, Development, and Succession	+ ⊘	= Treadmill; inertia; planning without action; a lot of talk and discussion; wasted effort
5	Leadership Capacity	+ Purpose and Values	+ Vision	+ Systems and Structures	+ ⊘	+ Execution	= Individual anxiety; high turnover because no development; lack of succession slows productivity
4	Leadership Capacity	+ Purpose and Values	+ Vision	+ ⊘	+ Selection, Development, and Succession	+ Execution	= Resistance, inefficiencies, duplication; growing relational tensions
3	Leadership Capacity	+ Purpose and Values	+ ⊘	+ Systems and Structures	+ Selection, Development, and Succession	+ Execution	= Lack of motivation; people at cross-purposes; initiative stifled
2	Leadership Capacity	+ ⊘	+ Vision	+ Systems and Structures	+ Selection, Development, and Succession	+ Execution	= Present success masks long-term conflict, confusion; no focus on common aproaches
1	⊘	+ Purpose and Values	+ Vision	+ Systems and Structures	+ Selection, Development, and Succession	+ Execution	= No unifying voice; drifting; fractious infighting; cynicism; gains in other areas eroded

FIGURE 40. THE SEVEN ELEMENTS OF AN ORGANIZATION AND THE THREE DIMENSIONS OF LEADERSHIP

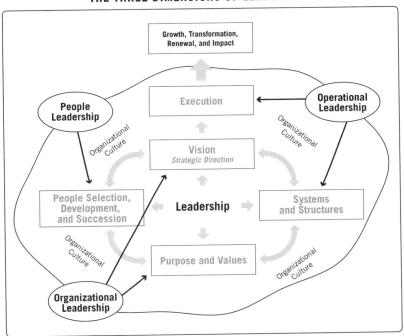

images capture the challenge of leadership, a challenge met with the appropriate application of the three dimensions of leadership. The remaining chapters explore these three dimensions in greater depth. And as you get your hands around these three dimensions, you will be like the sculptor releasing the angel from the block of marble.

8

THE PRACTICE OF ORGANIZATIONAL LEADERSHIP

Sustaining the Relevance and Impact of Your Organization

There's a story that's been around for some time about a man who stopped at a construction site to ask one of the workers what he was doing. The worker was chipping away at a large block of stone; taken aback by such an obvious question, he gave the obvious answer: "What does it look like? I'm chipping away at this stone." Walking on a little farther, the man asked another worker, doing the same job, the same question. "Look, Mister," came the reply, "I don't know about you, but I have a family to feed, and I'm here to put bread on the table." Walking on still farther, the man came to a third worker and asked him the same question. This worker stood up, stretched to his full height, and with a smile on his face and a gleam in his eye, replied, "Sir, I am building a cathedral."

Early on in my career, my wife and I lived in Strasbourg, nestled against the Rhine in the easternmost part of France. From our apartment balcony, you could see the city's famous cathedral in the distance, framed between two nearby modern apartment buildings. Even from that distance, it was an impressive sight, standing over 460 feet tall, with massive flying buttresses on either side and intricate carvings outside as well as inside, a striking blend of strength and refinement. It was started in 1176 and took almost three hundred years to build. The original architects never saw its completion, and most of its builders died on the job. It went through numerous setbacks—fires, political upheavals, wars, lack of funding—and yet there it stands, not only as a monument to human ingenuity but also as a reminder of the power of a clear and compelling purpose—strong enough to survive through generations.

The cathedral was a frequent reminder of the three construction workers. Which of the three do you think attracted the greatest loyalty? Which enlisted other people's talent most easily? Which was the most resourceful in overcoming challenges? Which was the most willing to take risks? Which was the most persistent in the face of setbacks and disappointments? It was, of course, the man with the clear sense of purpose—the man who understood he was really building a cathedral.

Such is the unifying, energizing power of a clear purpose, a clear vision, and strong values—the hallmarks of great leadership. These qualities are inherent in the three functions of organizational leadership:

- Creating and clarifying the direction

- Aligning the organization and its resources to that direction

- Selling and promoting the message of the direction

CREATING AND CLARIFYING DIRECTION

Karl Albrecht's *The Northbound Train* (1994) has a very simple premise: you need to know where your train is going. If it's going north, say so and give people the freedom to decide whether to climb on board. If they want to travel south, they won't ride your train. But they can't make that decision if you don't clearly state the direction.

Articulating the organization's direction, however, is not just a question of picking some goals and going after them, however big and audacious they are. It is much more about creating the kind of environment where the purpose, vision, and values (the PVV) are so clear that defining goals is almost a no-brainer, following a logic and consistency provided by the clarity of the PVV. Articulating the organization's direction is as much qualitative as it is quantitative, defining the organization's very essence, the unique way the organization sees itself, and the mark it's going to leave on the world, as discussed in Chapter 7.

Creating and clarifying direction, then, is about the why, the how, and the what of an organization. It spells out

- *Why* the organization exists (its purpose)

- *What* it wants to become in the future (its vision)

- *How* it goes about pursuing its purpose (its values)

Purpose defines the fundamental drive of the organization; values define how it will get there and how the members of the organization will behave when working toward that purpose, and vision defines what the organization will look like in the future if it reaches its goal. The following sections explore these in more detail. As indicated in Chapter 7, the order is interchangeable: purpose-values-vision or purpose-vision-values. In this chapter, the order is purpose-vision-values

Creating and Clarifying Purpose

Purpose is the starting point. And, in many ways, it's the hardest. The marketplace has been beaten to death with mission statements, and the cynicism toward these heavily constructed, supposedly inspiring sentences is at times almost palpable. At least, we console ourselves, they gave us Dilbert.

The depth of their misuse came home to me when, during a particularly heavy load of speaking engagements both in and outside the United States, I started asking the participants three questions. The first was How many of them worked for a company that had a publicized mission statement? Almost every hand would go up. The second question was How many could recite it for me? Almost every hand would drop. For the few, if any, remaining, I would ask the third question: Does it have an impact on the way you carry out your work? If a hundred hands were raised for the first question, I might be left with one for the third, often with none. More anecdotal than scientific, the exercise nonetheless indicated that for all the investment of time, energy, and money in formulating each mission statement, it was evidently having little impact . . . and in most cases, it was probably counterproductive.

The problem is not in the intent of the mission statement. Its intent is worthy: to bring clarity to the organization's fundamental purpose. Whether you call it *purpose* or *mission,* an organization needs it to be clearly defined, and defining it is a leadership function. If the leaders don't define it, it doesn't get defined.

Defining purpose, however, is hard work. Organizations are pragmatic enterprises, and defining their purpose requires a measure of their abstract thinking that stands in contrast to the concrete nature of their daily activities. Because many leaders who attempt to address the question find themselves in an area of discomfort, they fall into one of three traps:

■ They reduce the organization's purpose to the obvious immediate function of the organization.

■ They reduce it to a purely financial purpose.

■ They draft a statement that includes everything and everyone, and thus says nothing.

Virtually every business can redefine its purpose beyond its obvious function. A candle manufacturer provides an alternative light source, but in reality, its purpose is to create moods. Casting its purpose in such terms gives it the freedom to experiment with different kinds of candles—as many candles as there are moods—and even to think beyond candles. So if your purpose statement just describes what you do or what you make, it is probably a poor purpose statement—chipping away at stones, not building cathedrals.

The temptation to reduce the purpose to financial terms is the easiest trap to fall into. Improving shareholder wealth is a legitimate function, but it isn't a legitimate purpose. This isn't to say that profit isn't important—it is, and companies need to make a profit to survive—but making money is the reward for adding genuine value; it doesn't constitute the primary purpose of an organization. When an organization defines its purpose by its financial results, it unwittingly unleashes a self-absorption that ultimately spells its demise. It attracts people who want to put bread on the table, not build cathedrals. The following unimpressive examples come from companies that are highly visible and recognizable (at least currently):

> "To achieve enhanced, long-term shareholder value by building a strong operating company serving diversified markets to earn a superior return on assets and to generate growth in cash flow."

"We exist to create value for our share owners on a long-term basis."

"Our overriding objective is to maximize shareholder value."

"To maximize profits to shareholders through products and services that enrich people's lives."

Some organizations recognize the narrowness of a financial purpose, but fall short of the disciplined definition of the value they bring. In an effort to avoid leaving anyone out, they end up with bland, meaningless statements that capture just about everyone they have anything to do with—such as these (also from highly visible and recognizable companies):

"To serve our customers, employees, shareholders and society by providing a broad range of services and products [in our field]."

"Serve our customers, build significant value for our shareholders, and provide growth opportunities for our associates."

These examples tell us that a purpose statement

- Shouldn't be just about making money. Improving shareholder value is a necessary condition, but it's not a purpose.

- Is not a description of products or customers, although its primary beneficiaries or customers will be implicit, if not explicit. It describes something more than just the organization's impact on its customers and employees.

- Doesn't identify strategies for reaching its constituents.

So what makes a good purpose statement?

A purpose statement defines the organization's reason for being. It answers the question, Why are we in existence? If this organization didn't exist, what gap would be left unfilled? A purpose statement typically defines that contribution in one of three ways: a social contribution, a quality-of-life contribution, or an industry contribution.

In defining its reason for being, it captures the soul of the organization. While it doesn't have to be a highly motivational statement, it should give you a whiff of the passions that drive the organization.

It's much larger than the scope of the organization. In one sense, an organization's real purpose can never be fulfilled, because it's pursuing something much larger than itself. The purpose is therefore bigger than any single person or any single unit or the organization itself.

It is a communication tool. It creates a framework for focusing dialogue; everyone uses the same language, and a large measure of confusion is eliminated.

It is a decision-making tool. It provides a framework that allows people within the organization to make choices. As Stephen Covey points out, it is easier to say "no" when you have a higher "yes."

No wonder defining an organization's purpose is hard work! But those who expend the time and energy reap impressive dividends. When the National Institute for Learning Disabilities defined its purpose as "creating, nurturing and multiplying the environments that strengthen and build the competence and confidence of those who struggle to learn," it created a purpose much larger than the organization itself. Its leaders realized that they wanted to change the way people think—not just how those with learning disabilities think but also how everyone in general thinks about learning disabilities and how to treat them. They wanted to improve the whole educational process.

Here are some further examples that get much closer to defining the essence of the organization:

- For Johnson & Johnson, it's "alleviating pain," a purpose driven by a strong sense of social contribution.

- Merck is "in the business of preserving and improving life."

- Fannie Mae's purpose is to strengthen the social fabric by continually democratizing home ownership.

- Wal-Mart's purpose is "to give ordinary folk the chance to buy the same things as rich people."

- For The Pampered Chef, it's "to strengthen family life through shared meals."

- For Cargill, it's to improve the standard of living around the world.

- For 3M, it's to solve unsolved problems innovatively: "Our real business is solving problems."

Each of these companies is highly successful financially. But that's not how they define themselves.

Purpose, then, is defining the cathedral. Vision is deciding what it's going to look like.

Creating and Clarifying Vision

The National Institute for Learning Disabilities has been in existence for more than twenty-five years, faithfully and powerfully serving a narrow segment of the educational market. Several years ago, it decided to broaden its scope, convinced that its service was too valuable to keep to a limited market. As it set out on a quest to define its scope, its leadership landed on the daunting goal of one million students in therapy by 2020—what they later called their 2020 Vision. When they first explored its implications, they almost abandoned it, because it meant, among other things, going from 3,000 trained therapists to 125,000 therapists. But, before dismissing the goal, they asked themselves, What *would* it take to reach that number? As they considered what they would need to do differently, they suddenly realized that it wasn't totally unrealistic—it was a huge stretch, but not unrealistic. So they embraced the vision and it galvanized them. Everything they did was now put under the scrutiny of that vision. It was clear, compelling, and captivating. It changed the organization.

Visions energize. A vision exercises a magnetic pull that irresistibly engages people in its pursuit. It captures the heart and the imagination. The purpose stimulates the mind as it pushes the organization forward, but the vision warms the heart as it pulls the organization to its destination. It provides the passion and energy that sustain morale and maintain the momentum.

Vision is long-term, an alien concept in present-day corporate thinking. Three to five years is not long term. Vision asks where you want your organization to be in ten, fifteen, or twenty years—maybe even thirty years. The greater your responsibility, the more important it is to cast your vision far into the future. But at whatever level you lead, you still need to cast a vision and articulate the concrete description of the future you are striving for. For the head of a department, it may be just three to five years. For some CEOs, it's twenty years or more. Whatever your role, vision extends beyond your tenure (ideally, a long way beyond your tenure), which requires that leaders focus on the long-term health of the organization rather than on the success of their careers.

Vision doesn't predict the future; it shapes it. Every great accomplishment goes through two creations—its creation in your mind and its creation at your hands. The second, tangible, creation is virtually impossible without the first, mental, creation.

So, the vision you define for your organization is your first creation. However distant from its ultimate reality, the clear and compelling vision you cast in the present has a huge impact on the growth of your organization. This is about defining a future you believe in, a compelling future that genuinely drives you. It's about your definition as your first creation, which becomes a powerful guide for growth and change as you and your people bring your second creation into being.

We can understand the power of vision intuitively, but we can also know it empirically. A Harvard study, conducted by John Kotter and Jim Heskett over eleven years with 207 companies in twenty-two industries worldwide, found that companies with vision-led cultures significantly outperformed those without, and this translated into four key performance criteria (see Table 2).

On every count, the difference between organizations with a clear vision and those without is impressive. Increased revenue is four times the size with vision as without, expanded workforce is eight times the size, growth of the share price is twelve times the size, and the difference in improved net income is downright staggering. If leaders ever needed an argument to convince them that the pursuit of net income (profit) as a goal in itself is ineffective, it's right here.

It is not difficult to understand why vision is so powerful. Vision does something for leaders: it lends them charisma they never had before. They suddenly find it easier to recruit good people and retain them, they find their staff are more loyal, and they find their people are more productive. It's not that they actually become more charismatic; rather, the vision they set out captures the imagination of their people. Vision breeds commitment and persistence—the clearer the vision and the stronger the commitment to it, the greater the persistence in overcoming the inevitable setbacks and disappointments in the pursuit of that vision.

How do you go about drafting a vision? You engage the past, the present, and the future: that is, you draw from the past, you anchor the future in the present, and you sharpen the focus of your picture of the future with a clear long-term goal.

Draw from the past to define the future. "What's past is prologue," Shakespeare wrote. He's right. The past can reveal much about the future.

TABLE 2. THE POWER OF VISION

	With Vision	Without Vision
Increased Revenue	682%	166%
Expanded Workforce	282%	36%
Growth of Share Price	901%	74%
Improved Net Income	756%	1%

Omar El Sawy, a professor at the University of Southern California, conducted an interesting experiment. He divided thirty-four CEOs into two groups and said, "Think of things that might happen to you in the future." However, he gave one group an additional task: before thinking about the future, he said, "think of the things that have happened to you in the past." The revealing result was that the group tasked to look at their past first had future time horizons that were twice as long as the group that looked straight into the future.

There's something about knowledge of the past that gives confidence for the future. That's why West Point reminds cadets that they are all part of the "long gray line" that has marched through history ever since its inception in 1802, and why they revere the Grants, the Pattons, the Schwartzkopfs, and the many others who have taken their place in that long gray line. That's why we celebrate the Fourth of July: remembering more than two hundred years of history helps us look beyond the current four years of any administration to the future legacy of this nation.

Every organization has a history. Even a young organization reflects the history and the aspirations of the people or person who founded it. Every decision and every document it creates over the years tells something about the essence of the organization and the core drivers that shaped its early ethos. As a leader, become a historian, mining the early business plans, the minutes from critical meetings, and the articles or any other documents that give you clues about the aspirations of its founders.

The great value of looking back lies in bringing the organization back to its core. Growth and success for an organization bring more opportunities, and those opportunities typically elicit a reactive approach that in some cases is consistent with its past and in other cases isn't. Mining the past brings the core essence of the organization back into focus, and, at the same time, it traces the evolution of growing core competencies that may well shape a new and more appropriate direction. Either way, studying the past will bring clarity.

Anchor the future in the realities of the present. You cast your vision in the framework of the world you operate in. That doesn't mean you limit the scope of your aspirations; it means that your stretching and challenging long-term aspirations are anchored in the credibility and realism of the possible, if not the guaranteed.

Every organization has an external environment and every unit within that organization has an exernal environment. For the organization, it is the broader marketplace, and for the business unit, it is the organization as well as its particular piece of the marketplace. Hidden, or perhaps not so hidden, in the external environment are both opportunities and threats that hold the seeds of its future. As you assume the role of amateur futurist, you can track the trends in such areas as these:

- *The current social and cultural environment:* Changing generational and demographic trends—and the cultural values that change with them.

- *The economic environment:* Probable effects on your business of macroeconomic conditions such as inflation, unemployment, interest rates, the rise of China and India, and global energy conditions.

- *The technological environment:* Likelihood of new technology either making your business obsolete or forcing you to change the way you deliver your services.

- *The competitive environment:* Existing direct competitors and their market positions, current breeding grounds for future competitors, and potential growth of substitute products, services, or strategies.

- *The regulatory environment:* Pending political or legal actions likely to affect your product or service, or changing public perceptions that could create controls that currently don't exist.

Picture the future you want to shape. Strong visions lead to bold initiatives, and bold initiatives are expressed in bold goals—goals that capture the heart, mind, and energy of the organization. When Stanford set its goal to become the Harvard of the West, when Ford set out to democratize the automobile, when Wal-Mart (in 1990, when it was a $40 billion company), set its sights on becoming a $125 billion company by 2000, when Sony, in 1945, set itself a fifty-year goal of becoming the Japanese company most associated with changing the worldwide image of poor Japanese quality, and when the National Institute for Learning Disabilities, in 2002, set itself the goal of reaching one million students in therapy by 2020, each defined a goal that focused the organization's considerable energies in one direction.

Such goals are compelling. They get people's attention, and, what is more important, they unify. They are widely publicized and widely embraced. They stretch and challenge, but they remain at least 51 percent believable.

Such goals—what Jim Collins and Jerry Porras call BHAGs ("Big Hairy Audacious Goals")—need to be firmly planted in the soil of the organization's purpose and values. If they aren't, they will sound hollow and opportunistic. Although Wal-Mart's goal of tripling its revenues in ten years sounds suspiciously like an opportunistic and monetary goal, it was in fact driven by the company's purpose (giving the opportunity for ordinary folk to buy the same things as rich people), since higher volume would give it greater leverage in delivering on its purpose. Without that purpose it would indeed have been a questionable goal.

Even if a big stretch goal is credible and compelling, it is likely to be disruptive if it isn't anchored in a clear purpose, however engaging the goal might be. NASA is again a good example. The goal of "landing a man on the moon and bringing him back safely to earth by the end of the decade" captured the nation's imagination and galvanized NASA. Against considerable odds, NASA achieved its goal, but then it meandered through the following decades without a clear definition of what it was trying to accomplish. It had been given a BHAG without the context of a purpose.

Once you have the goal, you can provide the detail. Imagine your world with this goal accomplished and with the same detail you see in the present. Walk around, observe your organization—what do you see as you look ahead? What does it look like? What kind of technology and equipment do you see? What qualities characterize your people? How do they approach their work? What characterizes the relationships within your organization? What kind of talent pool do you have? What kind of customers do you have? What kind of relationships do you have with them? What kind of market share do you have? How do your financial statements read? What kind of reputation do you have in the industry? What kind of reputation in the community? How global are you?

Your vision has given you a destination point on the horizon; now it's time to make sure you get there.

Creating and Clarifying Values

Part of the Nordstrom folklore includes the story of an irate man who returned a set of defective car tires. Without batting an eye, the saleswoman gave him a full refund. That may not seem unusual, except that Nordstrom doesn't sell car tires. For many that response would be viewed as an act of stupidity, but, in the Nordstrom culture, it was held up as a model of great customer service—Nordstrom's one critical, driving value. It should be added that Nordstrom has estimated that at most 2 percent of its clientele will abuse its fanatical commitment to customer service, and it will not let the 98 percent suffer because of the 2 percent.

The most significant thing to me about the tire story (which, I'm assured, is not apocryphal) is that the saleswoman knew instinctively what to do. She didn't have to ask her manager what to do; she knew what to do because she knew, understood, and was led by the values of the organization.

Great leaders make the organization's values so clear that the values become the benchmark of behavior. "I firmly believe," wrote Tom Watson Jr. when he was CEO of IBM, "that any organization, in order to survive and achieve success, must have a sound set of beliefs on which it premises all its policies and actions. Next, I believe that the most important single factor in corporate success is faithful adherence to those beliefs. . . . Beliefs must always come before policies, practices, and goals. The latter must always be altered if they are seen to violate fundamental beliefs."

For Tom Watson, organizational success was about values or "beliefs." "Success and failure in a corporation," he said, lie "in the power of what we call beliefs and the appeal these beliefs have for its people."

Organizations are defined by their values. When you left one company to join another, chances are it was ultimately the values of the new company that sold you, albeit subconsciously, on the move.

The money may have been attractive, but something else clinched it. When you explained the move, you told people, "I like their focus on . . . " and you expounded on a value. The stronger the early impression of a positive value, the greater the sense of disappointment and deception if that value turns out to be an illusion. Conversely, you may be among the many to have turned down an offer, however financially attractive, because you didn't see yourself operating in that kind of culture with those kinds of values.

Organizations are also driven by values. Values give the organization substance and meaning; they determine how decisions are made, what kinds of people succeed, how customers and employees are viewed, and how power is distributed. Because values are so critical, effective leaders very consciously and deliberately shape the values they want to define the organization.

The reverse is also true: poor leaders have a weak grasp on values, and the organization ends up being led by whatever value is dominant at the time. Values may be unconscious and therefore unchallenged; there may be a dichotomy between stated values and actual values. A company may tout people development as a value, but fail to make the appropriate investments. A company may claim innovation as a value, but fail to tie performance rewards to innovative behaviors.

Values have to do with price. When leaders place a high value on certain behaviors, they are willing to pay a price to see them lived out—and they pay with the time and effort they take to model and encourage those behaviors.

In the 1990s, we saw much more attention paid to corporate values, and the attention came in large part from the growing interest in corporate cultures. Edgar Schein and others brought an anthropological perspective (though they didn't call it that) that naturally surfaced the often subconscious values that drive organizations. The research of Jim Collins and Jerry Porras reinforced the conclusion that enduring companies endure because of enduring values.

The need for a clear set of values is just as great for nonprofit organizations as it is for for-profit organizations. Nonprofits are more likely to think about the values they operate by, but many nonprofits hide behind their purpose and avoid a disciplined expression of their values. Further, nonprofits can be as mercenary as the most mercenary for-profit—and get away with it more easily.

Just what are values? Values are those principles that guide an organization. Over the past ten years, they have become a widely accepted concept in business and organizational development, as well as the subject of some significant research. Collins and Porras call them "essential and enduring tenets—a small set of general guiding principles," and, they warn, "not to be compromised for financial gain or short-term expediency."

Three kinds of values can be found in organizations:

■ *Operational values* determine the success of your particular business in your particular industry, whether the focus is, for example, on process excellence or innovation. Ultimately, when companies compete, they compete on the basis of their operational values.

■ *Work-environment values* identify those qualities you want to characterize your workplace—qualities of focus, interaction, and performance.

■ *Moral values* define the way you will pursue the operational values and work-environment values—with fairness, equity, respect, integrity, or whatever moral qualities you deem important.

Operational values are foundational values: they drive the organization. Work-environment and moral values are supporting values: they reinforce the operational values.

Defining operational values as foundational doesn't trivialize moral values. Moral values are critically important as support. If the operational values are unstated or unclear, the moral values have no context. If the moral values are unstated or unclear, the operational values will lack sustaining guidance.

Operational values. The core operational value you choose defines the way you compete in the marketplace. Because successful organizations are characterized by their strong commitment to one value more than to any other, their choice defines not only how they compete but also how they conquer. The stronger the value and the greater the organizational commitment to it, the easier it is for the organization to differentiate itself from, and surpass, its competition. These are the three main operational values:

TABLE 3. THE THREE OPERATIONAL VALUES

	Process Excellence	Product or Service Dominance	Customer Experience
Primary Focus	Process	Product or service	Customer
Customer Response	Response to great efficiency (and therefore lower cost)	Response to a great product or service	Response to a great experience
Role of Innovation	Focused on better processes and delivery mechanisms	Focused on better products/services	Focused on memorable customer experiences

- Process excellence

- Product or service dominance

- Customer experience

Some refer to these as primary strategies, but I prefer to think of them as values, because values generate more buy-in than strategies. Values have permanence; strategies come and go. Values capture the heart; strategies capture the mind. Table 3 shows primary focus, customer response, and the role of innovation for each operational value.

Process excellence requires an absolute commitment to improving the delivery process. It has to do with price, delivery, access, efficiency, safety, and speed. For a long time, it applied to manufacturing, but it certainly isn't limited to manufacturing. Wal-Mart applied it to retail: the retail giant pursued price competitiveness by developing one of the best inventorying systems in its industry.

Just about every industry (and every function within a business) is a candidate for process excellence, but it makes more sense for volume businesses with repetitive functions. Dell's competitive edge is process excellence. So, perhaps counterintuitively, is Disney's (at least the attraction side of the business). Its people are able to create a memorable customer experience because of their ability to efficiently process hordes of visitors through a certain number of attractions without snapping the visitors' patience. On the flip side, airlines that create a memorable experience but fail to provide on-time departures will lose customers; airline customers want to get to their destination on time, in one piece, and with their baggage intact more than they want a memorable experience.

Customer service, it has been said, is part smiles and part systems. Those who choose process excellence as a value recognize that the smiles come from the efficiency of their systems. If your systems are consistently poor, it won't be long before your smiles are useless.

In my late twenties, I ran one of the two French offices for a Dutch produce brokerage company. We bought produce from auctions in Holland and on the Rotterdam and Amsterdam port exchanges to sell to our high-volume clients, each of which bought truckloads of merchandise. We spent much of the early part of the business cultivating strong customer relationships; it paid off, because we had a solid roster of clients, and we worked hard at maintaining them. At one point we switched transportation companies to cut costs, and we found ourselves with angry customers whose produce hadn't arrived on time—not just an inventory issue, but also a price issue in what was often a highly volatile market. At that point, smiles didn't matter a great deal; the system had failed. We knew that if we didn't repair the system, we would lose the customers we had worked so hard to win. We promptly switched back to the original transportation company. It was clear that our competitive edge lay in process excellence.

Product or service dominance requires a high level of product differentiation and technological leadership, which, in turn, require creativity, product innovation, and strong first-to-market capabilities. The focus is on developing the best product or service in the industry and deploying it rapidly in the marketplace. 3M's strong focus on innovation created the kind of environment that gave birth to Post-it Notes and a host of other highly original products. Such companies' responsiveness is directed more to the market than to existing customers, looking for needs that haven't been met or even identified.

Customer experience provides the flexibility, adaptability, and customization that process excellence and product or service dominance cannot or will not provide. Focus on customer experience is most appropriate for project-based providers such as consulting firms, engineering firms, industrial and commercial construction companies, advertising agencies, and so on—any business where each project is

FIGURE 41. OPERATIONAL VALUES AS DIFFERENTIATORS

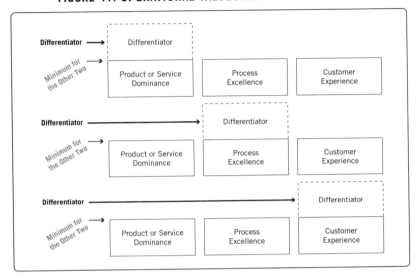

different and where the project is predicated on a high level of direct, continued interaction with the client. These companies know that people buy less on expertise and more on the way they experience the vendor. In contrast, companies like Dell, even though they offer a wide range of products and are constantly extending their product range, will not offer services beyond those that their delivery model can supply. This is why such process-excellence–oriented companies often struggle in their after-sales customer care—customers buy because of the price benefit from process excellence but are later disappointed by the limitations of customized attention imposed by process excellence

As you look at these operational values, you may be thinking that all three look pretty good. At some level, all three do need to be in effect, but the reality is that you can only be a differentiator in one (see Figure 41). If you try to stand out in all three, you will stand out in none, a fact supported by the research of the past fifteen years. (See Michael Treacy and Fred Wiersema's *The Disciplines of Market Leaders*, for example, as well as Michael Porter's *Competitive Advantage*.) Every marketing strategy needs to be shaped and inspired by the single core operational value your organization has chosen to pursue. Wal-Mart cannot afford to create unpleasant customer experiences, for all its focus on process. 3M cannot afford to ignore processes, for all its focus on product innovation.

TEN FACTS ABOUT VALUES

1. **Values define an organization's behavior. Identified or not, every organization has values.**
   An organization's behavior is the sum of its values—often unrecognized, nonetheless very real. When you move to a new organization, your adjustment is primarily an adjustment to its values.

2. **Values guide decisions.**
   Unconsciously, people use values to influence the way decisions are made. To uncover your company's values, assess the way it makes decisions. To get people to make the right decisions, teach them to embrace the right values.

3. **For every organization, some values are better than others.**
   Not all organizations embrace the same values, nor should they: what is good for one organization is not necessarily good for another. Good values do not have to be original, but they do need to be authentic.

4. **Strongly upheld and clearly articulated values free up an organization to creatively and flexibly pursue its purpose and vision.**
   Far from confining your organization, clear values actually set it free. They provide a framework for initiative. They provide the protective barriers that keep the organization from self-destructive behaviors, that is, from behaviors inconsistent with its purpose and vision.

5. **Many conflicts in an organization are rooted in unclear values.**
   Conflict is a healthy and normal part of your corporate growth, but conflict over values is much harder to reconcile. That's why many mergers fail. When Daimler-Benz and Chrysler engineers spent a week early in the merger arguing over the shape of a brochure, they weren't just arguing about brochures. They were also arguing about values.

6. **Leaders often have little trouble trusting people who share their values.**
   In reality, you can only empower people when you as the leader know that those you are empowering value what you value.

7. **Shared values generate trust.**
   By the same token, clear values give your people a structure and framework that make them feel secure.

8. **When an operational value conflicts with a moral value, let the moral value win.**
   Whatever your core driving operational value—process excellence, customer experience, product dominance—it will at some point conflict with your stated moral values. Don't sacrifice a moral value to honor an operational value.

9. **A clear sense of values simplifies the task of defining a meaningful purpose statement.**
Defining your values can help you define your purpose.

10. **Hiring most frequently focuses on talents and experience, with little concern for the person's values, setting up the possibility for a serious values crisis.**
If you wonder why you are having difficulties with a recent hire, it may be that the person has not bought into the values of your organization. Or, they may be challenging some values that should be challenged. If you are clear on your values, you will be able to tell the difference.

The effectiveness of an organization is thus shaped by its commitment to a core operational value and by its ability to let that value drive the business. When an operational value (or any other value, for that matter) is widely embraced, you don't need a thick manual to explain it. Nordstrom's commitment to its value of creating a powerful customer experience is so strong that all the instruction new employees get is a 5" × 8" card with statements such as, "We're glad to have you with our company. Our number one goal is to provide outstanding customer service. Set both your personal and professional goals high. We have great confidence in your ability to achieve them." The only rule is "Use your good judgment in all situations," with the encouragement "to ask your department manager, store manager, or division general manager any question at any time." Strength and clarity of values allows sparseness of text.

Effective organizations know how to incorporate their values into the structure of their organization. 3M's primary operational value is innovation focused on product dominance, and the structure reinforces the value. Under the company's "15-25-5 principle," technical professionals can spend up to 15 percent of their time on any project they want, and each division is expected to generate 25 percent of its profits from products developed in the past five years (since 1993, in the past four years). The structure reinforces the values.

The key thought about operational values is this:

Success comes from finding the right operational value to define your organization. You can realistically embrace only one. That does not mean that you abandon the others; it simply means that they support the core operational value that drives the organization.

Work-environment values. With your operational value defined, it becomes much easier to decide what kind of work environment you want to support it.

When you say to those around you, "We need to make this place more . . . " and you add an adjective, you have just expressed a work-environment value. This category covers areas such as performance standards, process style, professional development, relationships, teamwork, and atmosphere.

Work-environment values will be shaped in part by the nature of the business. Teamwork is less likely to be a value for a largely dispersed and solitary field staff than for an assembly unit.

More important, your work environment will be shaped by your purpose, vision, and values. The long-term goal you set will help define the kinds of qualities you are looking for in your workforce. So will your values. If your operational value is process excellence, you will look for certain qualities (such as project management skills, attention to detail, and responsiveness) that would be inappropriate for an organization whose operational value is customer experience, (which will look for qualities such as the ability to listen, connect, and communicate). How you measure performance, the kind of relationships that exist, the process style, the attitude toward training and development will thus be shaped by the operational value that defines your organization.

Your job as an organizational leader, then, is to make sure that the work-environment values that best support your purpose, vision, and values are identified and reinforced.

Moral values. Moral values are in fact work-environment values, but with a moral dimension. They define right and wrong within the workplace, and the list is short:

- *Integrity:* Honesty, truth, trustworthiness, forthrightness

- *Fairness:* Justice, equality of opportunity

- *Respect:* Recognition, consideration

- *Grace:* Forgiveness, compassion

That organizations today need to spell out moral values is in large part a reflection of a society in which moral values have lost widespread acceptance as absolute standards of professional behavior. A few generations ago, integrity and respect, for example, were considered normative, and it would not have occurred to an organization to list them as corporate values. Any discussion of such values focused on their violation, not their absence. Today, appealing to moral values is a marketing prerequisite: "You can do business with us—we are honest." "You can work with us—we treat people with respect."

Integrity is foundational. If you keep your word, you exercise integrity, and thus credibility; people will listen to you and trust you. Integrity breeds fairness. Fairness isn't treating everyone identically; fairness is treating people appropriately for their level of performance and behavior. Respect and honor appear in corporate literature. Many organizations are implementing respect training, although much of it is diversity training under a different title.

Grace may be the surprise value. Interestingly, grace figures high in strong cultures that reinforce moral values. The story is told of a senior executive at IBM who made a very costly mistake—to the tune of $10 million—a large sum by today's standards, and a huge one at the time it occurred, when IBM was still under the leadership of Tom Watson Sr. The executive came to Tom Watson with his resignation in hand, but was rebuffed by a remarkable statement along these lines: "What?! Do you think I'm going to let you go after I've just spent $10 million on your education?" Tom Watson understood the impact of grace and forgiveness.

An absence of grace, forgiveness, and compassion is particularly stifling in an organization that values innovation; in fact, innovation cannot survive without these qualities. One of my clients, a well-known company in its industry, placed a high value on keeping commitments. That may appear to be a laudable value, but the net effect was to keep people from making any commitments that contained the slightest risk of failure. Innovation and initiative were stifled.

Leaders are the guardians of the moral values, and yet this is where many leaders run aground: if they feel compelled to proclaim values they don't believe in, they create a serious disconnect between statement and practice. Better to not state values in the first place. But, best of all, state them and live them.

Never underestimate the power of values. They can be a powerful ally or a powerful enemy.

ALIGNING THE ORGANIZATION AND ITS RESOURCES

Alignment is the second function of organizational leadership.

As noted earlier, every organization is designed to fulfill two functions: make decisions and reward (or punish) those decisions. Between the decision and the reward, a series of processes either hinder or enhance the efficiency of the decision. The role of organizational leaders is to make sure that the process from decision to reward is aligned with the organization's purpose, vision, and values. To do so, leaders focus on

- Identifying the critical success factors

- Identifying the decision-making patterns

- Uncovering both the formal and the informal reward structures

The critical success factors (CSFs) are the crucial link between the aspirations expressed in the purpose, vision, and values and the execution lived out in everyday reality. With your purpose defined, your vision clarified, and your values crystallized, you can identify what is absolutely essential to the successful pursuit of your PVV. Typically, you will identify somewhere between five and seven critical success factors, and these factors will shape and define decisions. Any decision that doesn't contribute to a critical success factor should not be made. (More on critical success factors in Chapter 9.)

Decision making is an issue of power. Identify the decision-making patterns, and you can identify the power structure, whether formally or informally defined. The anatomy of organizational structure is the anatomy of its decision-making process. Power exists to make decisions, and, ultimately to reward (or punish) those decisions.

Decision making has two components: systems and structures (see Figure 42). What are the systems that guide how decisions are reached, and who is responsible for making them? The decision-making processes and responsibility structures generate rewards, which in turn reinforce the processes and structures.

Even in the most autocratic environments, decision making is not cut-and-dried; in fact, complicated political posturing is often hidden behind a seemingly monolithic structure. Decisions are thus seldom made in isolation: one person may decide, others may be consulted, others may need to be informed, and yet others may have to approve—not to mention the person who has to execute the decision.

This is the task of alignment. (More on this in the next chapter).

FIGURE 42. THE DECISION-MAKING PROCESS

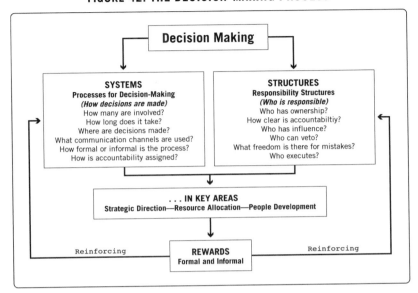

SELLING THE MESSAGE TO THE WHOLE ORGANIZATION

No matter how well you've succeeded at creating and clarifying the organization's direction, and at aligning the organization and its resources to its purpose, vision, and values, your job isn't finished—you need to sell the message to the rest of the organization and whatever other audiences need to hear it. To sell the message, you need to target your audiences and you need to manage the change process.

Targeting Your Audiences

An almost universal assumption that leaders make is that their message is being understood and embraced with the same intensity and commitment with which they themselves live it and speak it. That's a false and costly assumption. Organizational leaders need to think of themselves as election campaigners—when they are sick and tired of getting out the message, the message is finally beginning to take root.

Each message needs tailoring to each audience, and because different audiences hear your message in different ways, you need to pick the right channels. Clarify your message, tailor it to your different audiences, and pick the right channels—not that complicated, but it requires discipline and commitment.

As you craft your message, don't turn up your nose at sound bites. Advertisers learned long ago that products and companies need slogans. Nike tells us to "just do it," GE "brings good things to life," Southwest says we are now "free to fly around the country," and Chevy trucks are still "built like a rock."

In a world of unstable values and unclear trumpet calls, leaders need to master the art of the slogan. Whatever you call it—slogan, motto, catchphrase, tagline, sound bite—you need a succinct statement of your message, what you stand for and where you're going, as a potent communication tool. A slogan you believe in and live by enhances your credibility. In a world where the fight for credibility has become tougher than ever, a good, honest, slogan, may be just what you need.

Few leaders think of themselves as advertisers and PR agents. But that's what they are, selling the message of their purpose, vision, and values—their direction. It's the ubiquitous billboard, the radio jingle, and the TV ad that keep your message alive. Because your job is not only to create and clarify direction but also to sell it, a slogan that encapsulates the essence of your direction is a powerful tool. It doesn't have to be particularly original, though it needs to be easy to remember. More important, it needs to be authentic. And it needs to connect emotionally.

The mission of the March of Dimes is "to improve the health of babies by preventing birth defects and infant mortality." But what gets staff and volunteers out of bed in the morning is not the mission but the slogan: "Saving Babies, Together." It's a powerful slogan, emphasizing teamwork ("together") and inspiring heroism ("saving babies").

The more consciously defined and the more clearly articulated your slogan is, the more effective it is as a guide to action. People, in and out of your organization, will know what to expect from you. Rather than restricting initiative, it releases it. You'd be surprised what good things it brings to life. Just do it.

Managing the Change

A critical part of selling the message is selling the change. As change agents, leaders face one of their greatest challenges when it comes to helping people deal with and embrace the inevitability of change.

When people go through change, they typically cycle through five distinct stages, whether consciously or unconsciously:

- Denial

- Resistance

- Depression

- Exploration

- Commitment

Leaders themselves go through these five stages, but they typically forget that other people need time to go through them as well. Understanding these stages, and allowing time for them, makes change much easier to facilitate.

Let me illustrate these five stages with a story. Kathleen Kelley, the owner of a small Manhattan bookstore, suddenly finds her store's very survival threatened by the arrival of a megadiscount bookstore. The impact on her business is dramatic and evident (to everyone but her). Despite her vanishing clientele and emptying coffers, she blithely dismisses this massively uneven competition as "Nothing to do with us. It's big, overstocked, impersonal, and full of ignorant salespeople." She's in denial—denying not its presence, but its impact.

Slowly, however, it becomes clear that the impact is real and far from benign. She decides to fight back and enlists her boyfriend, a columnist, to write a column in defense of her bookstore. She gets the local TV news station involved and mobilizes a picket line. She has moved to resistance. (If this story is beginning to sound familiar, it's because you have seen *You've Got Mail*, with Kathleen Kelley portrayed by Meg Ryan.)

It soon becomes clear that resistance isn't working. The downward spiral of her business continues to its dismal conclusion. "People are always telling you that change is a good thing," Kathleen muses as she closes up the bookstore for the last time. "But all they are really saying is that something you didn't want to happen at all, has happened. . . . I'm heartbroken. I feel as if part of me has died. And no one can ever make it right." Everything looks very bleak. She's in depression.

New doors, however, open up: Kathleen starts writing a children's book, and she's offered a job as a children's book editor. There is still

FIGURE 43. THE FIVE STAGES OF CHANGE

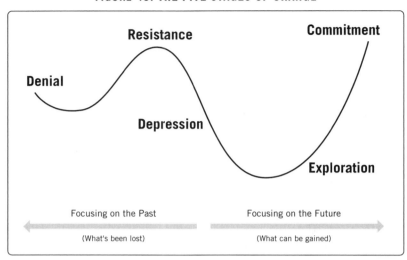

some confusion and the sense of loss hasn't been eradicated, but there is now a greater sense of hope and even excitement. She's exploring alternatives.

The new reality is far better than the reality she lost. But she needs time to recognize it and adapt to it. Kathleen's cycle through these stages is normal and healthy (see Figure 43). In fact often, change can only be fully assimilated by going through the whole process. In the final stage, she makes a commitment to a new life.

Unfortunately, many leaders have a hard time giving people time to process change.

Many leaders, even though they themselves wrestled through the five stages, expect their people to move straight to commitment without taking the time to work through the first four. They get discouraged by people's denial, resistance, and depression, and they may mistakenly see the reactions as permanent. Exploration is seen as a threat, not as the healthy process of taking ownership. But leaders who exercise patience and understanding are more likely to elicit support and cooperation. Their people will see that change, after all, can work out for the good—in their own lives, not just on the big screen.

The need for patience is all the more acute when we consider the reasons people resist change. These reasons have to do with perceptions—their perceptions of the change itself, of the change agent (the leader), and of themselves:

Their perceptions of the change itself:

- They don't understand it.

- They don't agree with the goal.

- They don't agree with the process.

Their perceptions of the change agent:

- They don't trust the change agent.

- They are cynical because of the history of past changes.

Their perceptions of themselves:

- They are afraid of failing (especially if rushed and pressured).

- They fear losing something they have a vested interest in (status, title, privileges, and so on).

- They don't want the additional work of relearning.

Some people are simply less flexible than others, and take longer to adapt to even the least threatening change. Some sources of resistance you can do little about, but many of them you can address. Identifying and understanding them will help you tailor your message to broaden and deepen your influence in the change process.

Leading change is a question of raising the desire for it. An insurance salesman once visited a remote farm, where a dog was quietly whimpering on the porch near the front door. When the farmer answered the door, the salesman asked him why the dog was whimpering. The dog was lying on a nail, he was informed. Why, he asked, didn't the dog get up and move? "Well," replied the farmer, "I guess because it doesn't hurt badly enough for him to want to move."

For many, the status quo doesn't hurt badly enough to want to change. In the end, leading change can be reduced to a simple equation:

$$\Delta = (De + Di + I) > C$$

Change (Δ) occurs when the desirability for the change (De), the level of dissatisfaction with the current status quo (Di), and the perceived likelihood of implementation (I) combine to exceed the cost of the change (C).

Leaders can influence the key variables in the equation. They can seldom do much to alter the cost of change, but they can often increase its desirability, they can increase the level of dissatisfaction with the current status quo, and they can convincingly push for implementation.

And that brings me neatly to the practice of operational leadership.

9

THE PRACTICE OF OPERATIONAL LEADERSHIP

Creating the Efficiencies of Your Organization

At some point, Peter Drucker once quipped, all planning has to degenerate into action. Operational leadership is about making sure that the planning doesn't stall and that the aspirations of the organization can be given some feet. Organizational leadership and operational leadership have a symbiotic relationship: organizational leadership brings disciplined thought to disciplined action, and operational leadership brings disciplined action to disciplined thought.

At the heart of operational leadership is systems thinking. Operations are about processes, and processes are part of systems. Some are recognized and conscious, some are unrecognized and unconscious. Remember, operational leadership is about identifying, planning, and shaping the processes that make up the systems, organizing them effectively, measuring their effectiveness, and solving problems revealed by the measurement.

Before examining these operational leadership functions, let's look at the connection between organizational leadership and operational leadership.

BRIDGING ORGANIZATIONAL AND OPERATIONAL LEADERSHIP

If you have ever been part of a corporate reorganization, you know that one of the biggest challenges leaders face is connecting the lofty aspirations of the future to the mundane realities of the present. That's why most mission statements, most expressions of corporate vision, and most values statements remain posted on the walls as guilty reminders of the credibility gap between the visions of the future and the experience of the present.

It doesn't have to be so. The link between present and future can be found in a clear identification of those elements—the critical success factors (CSFs)—that are essential to the fulfillment of the organization's purpose, vision, and values (PVV).

Whatever your organization, certain factors are essential to the successful pursuit of your purpose and the successful accomplishment of your vision. If critical factors are ignored, success will be at the very least compromised and quite possibly unachievable.

CSFs are an issue of leadership. They are key to embarking on any alignment and implementation strategy, every bit as important as the PVV itself, because they help define the behaviors of the functions of all three dimensions of leadership. (Table 4 reviews the functions of each dimension of leadership.)

At each level, critical success factors define leaders' roles:

- Organizational leadership organizes the alignment around the CSFs.

- Operational leadership organizes the systems and processes around the CSFs.

- People leadership (discussed in Chapter 10) organizes the skills and behaviors of the workforce around the CSFs.

The more all three dimensions of leadership are connected by both the PVV and the CSFs (see Figure 44), the stronger the leadership throughout the organization.

TABLE 4. THE FUNCTIONS OF THE THREE DIMENSIONS OF LEADERSHIP

Organizational Leadership (CAS)	Operational Leadership (POM)	People Leadership (SEM)
▪ **C**reating and clarifying the direction ▪ **A**ligning the organization and its resources to that direction ▪ **S**elling and promoting the message of the direction	▪ **P**lanning and shaping the process ▪ **O**rganizing and controlling ▪ **M**easuring and problem solving	▪ **S**electing and matching the right people ▪ **E**xplain and clarifying expectations ▪ **M**otivating and developing

FIGURE 44. THE THREE DIMENSIONS OF LEADERSHIP

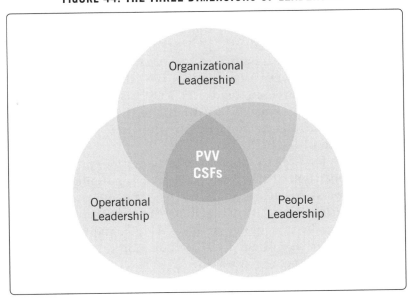

In some cases, the critical success factors are obvious, in others they are not. If you have done a good job of defining your purpose, your vision, and your values, the CSFs may need some digging up, but they won't be far below the surface (and if you haven't done a good job, trying to uncover the CSFs will be frustrating and meaningless, unless the attempt pushes you to clarify your purpose, vision, and values). When the National Institute for Learning Disabilities, for example, decided on its goal of one million students in therapy by 2020, it didn't take long for its leaders to uncover two CSFs: an adequate number of therapists and a high level of training sophistication. Both were critical to their success.

For a nonprofit scientific association, one CSF is its ability to access the particular body of scientific knowledge it specializes in and then disseminate it rapidly and reliably to those interested in the field. A freight company requires an adequate, reliable supply of drivers, the perennial bottleneck for the growth of a trucking company. A fleet management company will need a technological infrastructure and the project management skills of its staff to support it. For a construction management company, its relationships with subcontractors is a likely CSF, and general contractors that fail to build solid relationships with their subcontractors may find their success compromised, particularly in a strong economy where subcontractors have plenty of work choices.

These examples suggest that an organization will have only one or two CSFs; in reality, organizations typically have somewhere between five and seven. In some cases, a CSF may reflect an existing deficiency; but, even when the deficiency is rectified, the CSF will still be needed. If a strong technological infrastructure is needed, it will still be needed when put in place.

At least a few CSFs will be dictated by both your purpose and the particular operational value your organization is pursuing (see Chapter 8 for process excellence, product or service dominance, and customer experience as operational values). Wal-Mart's operational value of process excellence requires an unswerving commitment to cost control and process efficiency. Wal-Mart developed its sophisticated inventory system because it was identified as a CSF for that operational value.

Apart from linking PVV and execution, CSFs fulfill two important functions:

The critical success factors act as the framework for the goals and action plans that form the substance of any strategic plan. Strategic planning typically breaks down if it is anchored neither in the purpose, vision, and values nor in a clear set of well-defined critical success factors. If the CSFs aren't clear, any goals that are identified are likely to focus on the wrong opportunities. The CSFs thus close the loop on setting the direction while they open the loop on execution. They

FIGURE 45. FROM PVV TO EXECUTION

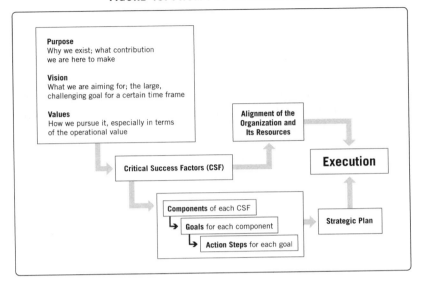

provide the pivotal link in getting from the PVV to the execution. The process is a cascading one: the PVVs cascade into the CSFs, the CSFs cascade into the components for each CSF, the components cascade into the goals for each component, and the goals cascade into the action steps for each goal (see Figure 45).

The critical success factors also act as the guide and the measure for the alignment of the organization and its resources with its purpose, vision, and values. When CSFs are clearly defined, alignment becomes a much easier process.

The critical success factors thus guide decisions and shape behavior. They become a defining framework—every bit as important as the purpose, vision, and values themselves.

Identifying Your Critical Success Factors

Identifying critical success factors starts with clarifying their nature. A critical success factor is a condition, and needs to be defined as such. What conditions are absolutely necessary for your purpose, vision, and values to become a reality? Look for the conditions that, if absent, will keep you from reaching the future you aspire to. The more you can qualify and clarify conditions without restricting them, the more useful they will be. These conditions may be internal or external; they may well be different from those pursued by a competitor, especially if the competitor is structuring itself around a different operational value.

If the purpose of a nonprofit organization cannot be accomplished without volunteers, an adequate supply of volunteers will be a critical success factor—a condition without which the organization cannot thrive or perhaps even survive. If the success of a trade show exhibits designer and manufacturer depends on the ability to master and integrate multiple communication media, that ability is a critical condition for the company. When an electronic components manufacturer is moving from commodity production to supply-chain-management services, the technology for real-time information is a condition without which it won't succeed.

Identifying Components

Once you have identified your critical success factors, you can identify components for each of them. At this stage, the tendency is to start identifying steps for implementation—tempting though that is, it's premature. At this stage, look for components, not action plans.

Consider the components of a well-functioning car:

■ The wheels (which allow it to move smoothly)

■ The engine (which provides the power)

■ The transmission (which connects the engine to the wheels)

■ The fuel (which provides energy to the engine)

■ The steering (which maintains the direction)

■ The foot pedals (which allow you to accelerate and brake)

■ The chassis and the body (which hold it all together)

Each of these is critical; without them the car either won't move or won't stay on the road. The list doesn't indicate a necessary order for the components; it just includes the components that are necessary. Addressing these components in the right sequence will depend on your purpose.

Imagine you are the owner of a NASCAR team, a relatively recent entrant to NASCAR, and eager to make your mark. Your goal is winning the championship in the next nine to twelve years. Your three-year goal is to be in the top ten, and your six-year goal is to be in the top three. Your critical success factors would at least include having the right car, having the right driving talent, and having the right backing. Each of these can be broken down into separate components (as for the car). By breaking a goal down into components, you can assess the relative importance of each component and the trade-off given the ultimate goal (winning the championship). In the example of the car, your goal and context will help you make decisions as you weigh the components. More fuel capacity in the car, for example, means fewer pit stops but a heavier load.

Virtually any critical success factor can be simplified by breaking it down into its essential components. A friend of mine had a high school football coach who claimed that if everyone did exactly what they were supposed to, every play would at least be a first down, if not a touchdown. As we pondered his claim, we identified five components to a successful football team:

- *Flawless execution:* This is the point the coach was making, but it's not alone.

- *Strategy:* One coach can out-coach another with a better strategy. Football can resemble a military encounter or a chess game. Someone calculated that in an average football game of three hours and eight minutes, the ball actually moves for only twelve minutes (that's about 6 percent of the time). The rest is strategy and planning.

- *Talent:* You can execute flawlessly, but the other team may be faster, stronger, more responsive, and more flexible. The other team may have a quarterback who can thread a needle the way your quarterback cannot.

- *Psychology:* You can execute flawlessly, have a better strategy, and have greater talent—and still not believe you will win.

- *Luck:* You can't plan for the bounce of the ball, a player losing his grip on a wet surface, or a poor refereeing decision.

Any critical success factor can be broken down into components. A CSF will have several components, each of which makes a unique contribution to that particular CSF. For a nonprofit organization dependent on an adequate supply of well-trained volunteers, key components would include recruitment, training, and retention. For creative design work, key components might include hiring creative designers, retaining them, and creating an atmosphere that rewards creativity. For supply chain management in a manufacturing plant, components might include raw material inventory management, production capacity management, inventory control, and manufacturing flexibility.

The more succinct a component, the more helpful it is. Identifying components is important because each component becomes the context for drafting specific goals the organization is going to pursue.

Identifying Goals

Once you have identified the components of your critical success factors, you are ready to list all the possible goals that relate to the components of a particular CSF. Take each component in turn and brainstorm possible goals related to it. You can categorize them by the different functional areas or departments that contribute to that component. Some departments or functional areas may contribute only a few goals. Others may contribute many.

If hiring creative designers is a component of the CSF "capacity for unusually creative designs,"a goal for that component might include defining the selection criteria for designers. Another might be to identify related industries known for their creativity as a possible source for hiring. Southwest Airlines recruits many of its flight attendants from the entertainment industry, unlike the rest of the airline industry. For a company that identifies manufacturing flexibility as a component of the CSF supply chain management, possible goals might include reducing product cycle time or line changeover time.

You will most likely come up with far more goals than you can reasonably execute. So now you need to prioritize them. Some you may discard, and some you may put on hold.

Make sure the goals you focus on are "Power" goals (see Figure 46). A well-articulated goal has extraordinary power. President Kennedy's 1961 moon speech became famous because he articulated the goal of "landing a man on the moon and bringing him back safely to earth by the end of the decade." It was an extraordinarily powerful goal.

The power of the goal lay in its deceptively clear articulation and definition. As Denis Waitley has pointed out, if Kennedy's goal had been "to beat the Russians in the space race" or "to create the best

FIGURE 46. POWER GOALS

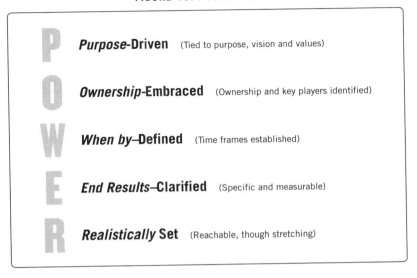

P   *Purpose*-**Driven**   (Tied to purpose, vision and values)

O   *Ownership*-**Embraced**   (Ownership and key players identified)

W   *When by*–**Defined**   (Time frames established)

E   *End Results*–**Clarified**   (Specific and measurable)

R   *Realistically* **Set**   (Reachable, though stretching)

space program," it would most likely have been ignored. Instead, it defined a time frame and clear results, and it was realistically set, even though extraordinarily challenging. Ownership was enthusiastically embraced.

It was a Power goal—almost. The one ingredient it lacked was being tied to a clear purpose for NASA, and NASA's later misadventures illustrate the importance of this point. NASA had a goal but it was unclear on its overall purpose as an organization. Did it exist primarily for military defense? Or for commercial and scientific exploration?

But, with your purpose and vision clear and your values meaningful, you will not fall into the same trap. In fact, you now have the makings of a strategic plan—and it will be a meaningful strategic plan, because it will be anchored in your purpose, vision, and values and in the critical success factors that flow out of them. To convert the CSFs, along with their relevant components and the goals that flow out of these components, into a strategic plan, you need to take a few more steps:

■ *Create action steps where necessary.* Applying the Power criteria to the goals may reveal that you need to take some specific action steps to reach the goals.

- *Assess the impact of each functional area on the CSF.* How important is each functional area—production, for example, or engineering, design, accounting, or human resources—to this CSF?

- *Identify the strengths that could promote this CSF and the obstacles that could handicap it.* Strengths and obstacles might lie in the technology and the equipment, or in the processes and work patterns, or in the management style of the leadership, or in the attitudes and assumptions of the people most closely associated with it.

- *Assign a champion to each CSF.* It doesn't have to be the person whose functional area is most closely related to the CSF, but it usually makes sense if it is. If the CSF, for example, is building a strong corps of highly creative designers, the HR director or the head of design would be a logical champion. The production manager would be less logical as the champion, unless you are deliberately cross-training and cross-fertilizing. Because champions are responsible for the success of the CSF, they need to be strongly endorsed and adequately resourced.

CSFs and the goals they generate are not simply more work piled up on top of everything else everyone needs to do. They *are* the work everyone needs to do. If people are doing something unrelated to a CSF, they shouldn't be doing it, unless that activity reflects a CSF that has been inadequately defined.

THE PREMISES FOR OPERATIONAL LEADERSHIP

Looking at the three functions of operational leadership, the POM functions—planning and shaping processes, organizing and controlling, and measuring and problem solving—uncovers the following premises:

The goal of operational leadership is to make sure that all the processes and decisions within the organization further rather hinder the pursuit of the PVV. Implied is a clear commitment to

- The organization's purpose

- The customers it is seeking to serve

- Its vision

- Its values

- Its critical success factors

Operational leadership keeps in mind that execution and implementation are undergirded by a constant and genuine focus on the customer— both the immediate customer of a particular process and the ultimate customer. Great execution starts with a clear understanding of what the customers really want and what they think constitutes great service.

Operational leadership is based on a solid understanding of systems thinking. The focus is on the processes, the heart of execution. If you master processes, you master execution. When the systems and processes are doing what they should be doing, they fulfill a few key deliverables:

- Increasing customer satisfaction

- Decreasing cycle times

- Decreasing the number of defects, glitches, or problems in the products or services

Operational leadership values data. As far as possible, the process is driven by facts and data. Facts and data don't eliminate intuition and well-founded hunches, but they impose a healthy discipline on them and they help keep intuition and hunches from inevitable errors of judgment.

Operational leadership doesn't rest on current success. Its mind-set is characterized by a constant search for improvement in all the key processes, however well they are currently functioning.

Cross-functional collaboration is critical to strong operational leadership. Cross-functional connectedness recognizes the interconnectedness and interdependence of every part of the organization.

Near-perfection in the process is the goal. At the same time, tolerance for failure is high, especially for failure that is the product of testing and experimenting for improvement.

Measurement is inherent to execution. Once the process has identified the customer and what that customer wants, it measures the effectiveness of its delivery by objective standards that reflect progress in meeting customer expectations. It's harder to solve any problem if you don't have a way of measuring progress.

With these premises in mind, it becomes feasible to define systems thinking.

The Importance of Systems Thinking

Systems are everywhere. We are subject to the vagaries of changing weather systems, which in turn can disrupt the delicate system of air traffic patterns. Disrupted transportation systems may affect the traveler's nervous system, which in turn may disrupt the digestive system. Strong weather systems can impact economic and social systems, sometimes severely. Economic and social systems affect each other, and both can be affected by subsystems within each one. Within the global economic system, for example, a macroeconomic development in one country can change the economic performance of another. Social and ecological systems influence, and are influenced by, other systems. Systems can be as small as the DNA system, or as large as the solar system, which is part of a still larger galactic system. Systems are everywhere.

The lesson of systems thinking is interdependence: systems create linkages that are far stronger than we imagine. "Systems thinking," Peter Scholtes tells us in *The Leader's Handbook,* "refers to the general reflex of conceiving reality in terms of interdependencies, interactions, and sequences." "At its broadest level," Peter Senge explains in *The Fifth Discipline,* "systems thinking encompasses a large and fairly amorphous body of methods, tools, and principles, all oriented to looking at the interrelatedness of forces, and seeing them as part of a common process." "Everything affects everything else in one way or another," states John Woods in *Work in Progress.* "Whether you are aware of that or not does not change the fact that this is what is happening. . . . A business is a system . . . and when you see it this way, you can manage your business better." Systems thinking allows us to acknowledge and anticipate the ripple effect of every choice we make and every initiative we undertake.

Thinking of organizations in terms of systems is the most logical approach to the implementation and execution of purpose, vision, and values. It took a while, however, for systems thinking to be applied to organizational performance; for much of the past century, organizations were viewed as essentially mechanistic entities that could be directly controlled and shaped. Pull one lever and you get one result; pull another and you get a different one. After World War II, however, thanks to the thinking of people like W. Edwards Deming, people began to look at organizations as more fluid, biological entities, whose growth and development were for the most part invisible and thus largely undetected.

In this paradigm, organizations are not just a function of the boxes in the organization chart; they are also a function of the lines, what happens between the boxes. In reality, what happens between the boxes is usually more significant than what happens inside the boxes, unless the people in the boxes know how to influence what happens beyond their box.

Powerful though they are, the systems of an organization can be shaped and influenced by the leadership to reinforce its aspirations. Deming himself, who was often accused of downplaying the human factor, saw the importance of leadership: "Institute leadership. The aim of leadership should be to help people, machines and gadgets do a better job." Systems thinking is shaped by values. Although Deming didn't use the term, in essence he was teaching values. What you value, you reward and reinforce, and what you reward and reinforce shapes behavior. And shaping behavior is a leadership function.

The understanding of systems is an evolutionary development. The first serious, formal measurement of processes began with statistical process control, a concept formalized in the 1920s by Walter Shewhart, who laid the foundation for a systematic approach to measuring variations from an identified and desirable mean. He contributed the control chart, which from his time onward became ubiquitous in any effort to measure quality. Systems thinking took a quantum leap forward with Deming (one of Shewhart's protégés), who was largely ignored in the United States but widely revered by the Japanese for his influence on their postwar resurgence.

With time, statistical process control became more sophisticated. Although later superseded by other process measurement and control models, it endured as the backbone of most of what followed. As a defensible oversimplification, in the two decades that followed World War II, the United States focused more on measuring human performance, and the Japanese focused more on process improvement.

When the Japanese juggernaut rolled into the American market in the 1970s, American companies began to look closely at process improvement. TQM (total quality management), a term coined by Bill Creech and presented in *The Five Pillars of TQM*, became the first serious model, largely a response to the perceived strengths of Japanese business. TQM took an incremental approach to quality improvement, drawing heavily on the legacy of statistical process control and measuring quality in terms of the product. "Product," Bill Creech noted, "is the focal point for organization purpose and achievement. Quality in the product is impossible without quality in the process."

TQM made sense at the time, and it made more sense when it was clear what the customer wanted, but it was later displaced by Six Sigma, which shifted the emphasis by applying a focused attention on customer needs: you can develop a great product with great processes delivering the product, but if the customer doesn't want it, the quality of the product and the processes delivering it are meaningless.

It was BPR (business process reengineering), however, that eclipsed TQM, and it did so because it took a macro look at processes, forcing an organization to look at the overall impact of its processes and not just their individual efficiency. "The key word in the definition of reengineering," Michael Hammer wrote in *Beyond Reengineering*, "is 'process': a complete end-to-end set of activities that together create value for a customer." BPR brought a further, much-needed, shift in focus, but it wound up in the center of controversy when for many organizations reengineering became the code word for downsizing.

The balanced scorecard, initially developed by Harvard's Robert Kaplan and consultant David Norton, also took a macro look at processes, attempting to integrate financial measures with customer impact, internal processes, and internal learning and growth. It was a conceptually tidy and well-constructed model that proved difficult to implement. Its track record suggests that where it failed, it failed not so much because of its macro approach but because companies were unclear on their purpose, vision, and values, and without them, the balanced scorecard was a structure without a foundation. Without a clear purpose, a clear vision, and a strong set of values, financial measures had no context, customer focus was unclear, internal processes were disconnected, and learning had no direction.

Six Sigma at a micro level became the dominant model. First developed at Motorola by Mikel Harry, it focused on a more incremental approach to process improvement. It was given a huge boost when Jack Welch and Larry Bossidy became its champions at GE and AlliedSignal respectively. And with good reason: well applied, it can generate a 10 percent net income improvement with every sigma shift, delivering the improvement by dramatically lowering the cost of quality.

Six Sigma elevated process improvement because of two substantial differences: it started with a clear focus on the customer, identifying what the customer really wanted; and it set a very high target,

TABLE 5: THE SIX SIGMA BENCHMARK FOR MEASUREMENT

Level	Defects (per million opportunities)	Yield (percent)
6	3.4	99.9997
5	233	99.98
4	6,210	99.38
3	66,807	93.32
2	308,537	69.15
1	690,000	30.85

near perfection, for the processes needed to deliver what the customer wanted. Its appeal lay in this twofold focus on the customer and on quantifiable and demanding performance measurements.

Six Sigma was thus a statistical measure of the performance of both the product or service and the process. Its meaning comes from the Greek letter *sigma* (Σ), used to describe standard deviation (how much variation exists in a set of data, a group of items, or a process).

Six Sigma's basic measurement is "defects per million opportunities," identifying six levels of performance. A million opportunities may be far more than a particular organization handles, but it creates a benchmark for measurement (Table 5).

A performance goal of 3.4 defects per million opportunities, or a yield of 99.9997 percent, is a pretty high standard, and few obtain it. But it underscores the importance of measurement and the value of a high standard. Whether it's Six Sigma or something else, process improvement needs to be measurable and measured.

The flaws of Six Sigma will doubtless be given greater exposure as our understanding evolves. Even at GE, a focus on innovation is challenging the once-preeminent role held by Six Sigma. But the need for focus on process efficiency remains. Any process improvement is a serious undertaking, especially one that combines a macro with a micro approach—the only kind that ultimately works. And that's what operational leadership is about—providing the impetus to plan and shape the processes of the organization; organizing the processes around the purpose, vision, and values, and the critical success factors; and applying the appropriate measurement and problem-solving methodologies.

The Big Picture of Systems Thinking

Conceptually, systems thinking is not complicated. It's actually quite intuitive. It starts by identifying the customer, which at a macro level has already been defined by the purpose and vision of the organization. It has been best represented by what has come to be called the SIPOC model: Suppliers—Inputs—Processes—Outputs—Customer.

The SIPOC model determines what the customer wants, expressed as outputs from the processes designed to deliver them; processes are fed by inputs, delivered by suppliers (see Figure 47). For the analysis, the process goes from right to left (backward); for the delivery, it goes from left to right (forward). To work well, the model requires a feedback mechanism that makes sure the customer is getting the desired outputs, and that the suppliers, inputs, and processes are delivering what the outputs require. The bulk of the focus is on the processes, once the outputs are clearly established.

The SIPOC model can and should be crafted at a macro level: every process has a customer. But it can and should be applied at a micro level, too: that process should deliver the outputs that best serve that customer.

Knowing what micro levels to address, however, requires a look at the macro tensions within your particular organization. Every department is in some way a supplier providing inputs into the processes that ultimately deliver the outputs your customer wants. Marketing, sales, business development, production, safety, production engineering, research and development, new product development, customer service, finance, information systems, human resources, each provide an input into the process that delivers the output. For a nonprofit organization, the list will include volunteer and member relations, fundraising, publications, and so on.

Whatever the organization, the role of operational leadership is to figure out the interdependencies of the inputs and identify ways that their contributions to the processes can produce a better output for the customer. In doing so, operational leaders pay particular attention to the transition points, where systems are weakest and where most processes fail. Relay teams are most vulnerable in the hand-off; so are the processes of an organization.

The Application and Implementation of Systems Thinking

Systems thinking is about mapping out and reshaping processes. My purpose here is not to provide you with a detailed methodology

FIGURE 47. SIPOC MODEL

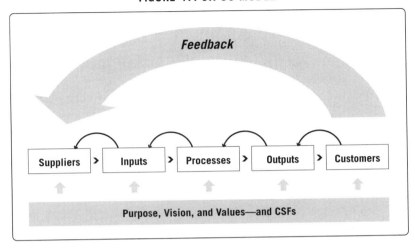

—plenty of resources already do that well—but to highlight some key considerations.

Selecting focus. Mapping out the processes of an organization is a daunting task, and not every process will be worth mapping. One criterion for selection is to go for the low-hanging fruit—the processes that have the highest yield and the greatest ease of implementation related to the most important products or services. But how do you recognize the low-hanging fruit?

The more important questions are What does this organization mean by high yield? How do you determine which are the most important products or services? Do you define importance in terms of the product's or service's contribution to the purpose, vision, and values? Or in terms of its cost-effectiveness? Or in terms of its growth potential?

Importance is defined by all three criteria, which allow you to assess every product or service you offer:

- What is its contribution to the organization's purpose, vision, and values?

- What is the cost and profitability associated with its delivery?

- What is its growth potential?

Your stars are those products or services whose contribution to your purpose and vision is unquestioned, whose cost is low, whose profitability is high, and whose growth potential is strong. Products that make little contribution to your PVV, that lose money, and that are stagnant are the obvious choices for sunsetting and elimination. Between the two ends of this spectrum are all your other products or services, which need more scrutiny. A training organization, for example, may have been carrying a flagship training program for years, even though it loses money and its enrollments have fallen off, raising serious questions about its growth potential. Because its contribution to the purpose and vision is still strong, the program would be a good candidate for process mapping, to look for process improvements that could raise its profitability and boost its appeal. If the process mapping yields no improvements, it's time to make the tough decision to keep it or eliminate it.

Harder still to decide on are products or services that are highly profitable and visible but don't fit your purpose and vision. You may be tempted to keep them in their present form because of the cash they generate. Process mapping helps you see if the product or service can be realigned to the organization's purpose and vision; if it can't, you can release it so its resources can be redirected to other efforts with a better match to the three basic criteria.

These comments have addressed the outputs to the customer, but they apply equally well to any service provided internally. Finance, marketing, and human resources all deliver services internally, and each service delivered to internal customers can be measured by the same criteria: its contribution to purpose, vision, and values; its cost-effectiveness; and its growth potential or usefulness.

Identifying roles. You need a champion: someone dedicated to the process, someone with project management capability, someone who can keep ad hoc teams focused on the processes they are addressing. You also need someone with acknowledged authority. Without a visible, accountable leader in this role, the implementation process will most likely flounder.

You need a sponsor—ideally, the CEO. More than anyone else, the CEO can give teeth to the process. If Jack Welch and Larry Bossidy hadn't provided fervent, vocal sponsorship for the process improvement implementation in their companies—even realigning bonuses to stimulate commitment—there is little likelihood that it would have gained much traction. Sponsorship is not just enthusiastic endorsement; it also provides the resources that the implementation needs: money, people, and training.

You need implementation teams, with members chosen either because of their direct or indirect involvement or because of their experience in the process issue the team is addressing. You need, of course, team leaders, chosen for their experience or exposure to the issue and their proven ability to lead a team effectively.

Applying the discipline of analysis and implementation. Scientific analysis is a highly disciplined process. If it weren't, you couldn't trust the results. Business process analysis, although perhaps not to the same degree, still requires a high level of discipline. Not without reason, Larry Bossidy and Ram Charan subtitled their book *Execution,* "The Discipline of Getting Things Done." Six Sigma expressed this disciplined approach in the DMAIC model: Define—Measure—Analyze—Improve—Control. Mikel Harry, the developer of Six Sigma, added "recognize" at the front end, and "standardize" and "integrate" at the back end. But the core essence is in defining, measuring, analyzing, improving, and controlling.

Defining is about identifying the problem. In some cases, the problem is obvious; in others, it isn't. You also need to clarify how this problem is affecting the outputs the customer is looking for. Identifying the problem and clarifying its impact allows you to figure out what will bring greater satisfaction to the customer of the process, and to define what the process will look like once you align it to the requirements of the customer. At a very different level, you'll also be defining how you will operate as a team, bringing clarity to the outcomes of your work together.

Measuring is about gathering data. This step requires restraint; it's tempting to jump to conclusions, but without the data, your conclusions may be based on false assumptions. This is where you map out the processes as accurately as you can. You focus on what is, not on what should be. The formula is simple:

$$Y = f(Xs)$$

where Y represents the outputs or outcomes, and X represents the inputs and processes, and the outputs are a function of the inputs and processes. You are measuring the X's—the inputs and processes.

Analyzing is what you've been itching to do all along and can now do with a reasonable expectation of drawing some solid conclusions. This is gap analysis: you are determining why you have a difference between what is and what should be. It may have to do with equipment and infrastructure; it may have to do with the way the process is handled. It may have to do with materials, or faulty measurements, or human error. But you have to analyze more than what the current problem is; you also have to analyze the impact the problem is having. Analysis allows you to quantify the problem and put a number on it; once you have that number you can measure whether you're going in the right direction. By analyzing the number of delivery errors, for example, the warehouse can measure progress in eliminating the errors, once it understands where the errors are coming from.

Improving is about action. Once your analysis has identified the difference between what is and what should be, and how to close the gap, you can implement changes. Once you have implemented them, you can test them and improve them. The greatest danger is settling for obvious assumptions and obvious remedies, without exploring different perspectives and without identifying creative or even radically different solutions.

Controlling is about maintaining the improvements or gains your changes initiated. Controlling involves developing a monitoring process so that old habits don't resurface and new habits don't die. It involves establishing a process for anticipating problems. By establishing a response mechanism for the problems that will inevitably arise, you reduce the risk of the improvements you have initiated being derailed.

Systems thinking comes with an abundance of tools. You may need to use only a few of them, but operational leaders who want to exercise a level of systems-thinking competency will want to develop some familiarity with all of them. The tools include check sheets, spreadsheets, flow charts and process mapping, cause-and-effect diagrams (fishbone, for example), scatter diagrams, responsibility charting, sampling techniques, frequency plotting, reward structure analysis, force field analysis, run charts, and many others.

Systems thinking and process alignment can be hard work. Is it worth it? Yes! The value is not just in improved results at the other end, the focus on what the customer really wants. The value is also in the discipline it instills: it makes you validate with data, not argue from hunches. It imposes the discipline of driving for root causes. It builds on what works, rather than focusing on what doesn't. It breaks old habits. It shifts the focus of performance measurement from inputs to outputs. It increases the likelihood of sustaining change because it makes change feasible and profitable. All told, as an operational leader, you have good reasons for embracing systems thinking.

THE KEYS TO GREAT EXECUTION

This chapter has been about the functions of operational leadership: planning and shaping processes, organizing and controlling, measuring and problem solving. But it has also been about the principles that undergird these functions, which are significant yet simple.

1. *Maintain a constant connection to the purpose, vision, and values.* The functions of operational leadership are at their most effective—in fact, they only have meaning—when they are connected to the purpose, vision, and values. There's another reason this connection is important: from a personal career perspective, the stronger the connection you maintain to the purpose, vision, and values as an operational leader, the easier you will find the transition from operational to organizational leadership (the notoriously difficult transition addressed in Chapter 6).

2. *Maintain a clear commitment to the critical success factors.* The CSFs are the measurement of operational performance. Whatever operational leaders pursue and achieve must be measured against the the critical success factors. Operational leaders are the guardians and champions of the CSFs every bit as much as the organizational leaders are.

3. *Develop a solid understanding of systems and process thinking.* Operational leadership is about systems and processes—understanding them, planning them, shaping them, and refining them. Effective operational leadership requires at least a minimum level of mastery in systems thinking.

4. *Intentionally connect execution to people development.* Process isn't everything. Systems and processes are a critical component in the overall chain shown in Figure 48—not the only one, but a critical one. They help guide and shape the way people are developed, and the way people are developed in turn reinforces the effectiveness of the systems and processes. The need for systems and processes to be clearly tied to the way people are developed is important for a very simple reason: you need people to run processes. Deming argued that there is no such thing as bad people, only bad processes; he may have been simply overstating the case to make a point. He clearly believed in the value of

FIGURE 48. THE RELATIONSHIP OF SYSTEMS AND
PROCESSES TO THE PVV AND PEOPLE DEVELOPMENT

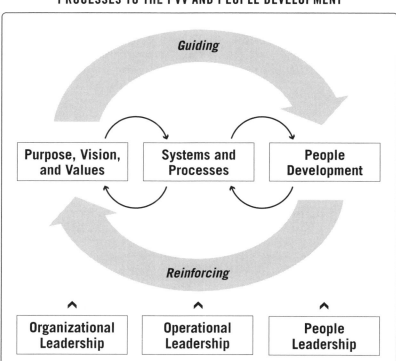

training, and if processes were not dependent on people, training would be superfluous.

So process isn't everything. You need people to run processes. . . . Which brings me to the critical dimension of people leadership. Once you have established the most effective and efficient systems and processes within your organization, you have done well. But now your task is to bring out the best in your people—without whom your processes will never deliver the full results they could deliver and that you want them to deliver. When you focus, not just on the processes, but also on the people who live in them, you're reinforcing organizational leadership with people leadership. And planning won't degenerate into action (in the words of Peter Drucker)—it will regenerate action.

10

THE PRACTICE
OF PEOPLE
LEADERSHIP

Bringing Out the Best in Your People

John is the operations manager for one of the business units of a large commercial construction company. Before he became operations manager, he was asked to take over a project that had turned sour and needed help. At risk was not only a long-standing client whose patience was wearing thin but also the company's reputation in the market.

Early on, he took the client out to lunch. "Sometimes on Saturdays," he told the client, "I put my young son in my pickup truck and we take a drive through this great city. As we go, I point out all the buildings I've helped build. I point out this one and that one [he named different landmarks—many impressive and well known]. You know something—I never point out this one right here. My son doesn't know I'm working on this project. And the reason I don't tell him is that I don't feel good about it. And I don't feel good about it because of the way we work on this project. I don't feel good about the relationships. I don't feel good about the way we work as a team. And what I've realized is that the buildings I'm proud of, I'm proud of because of the people that I've worked with on them. And that's what I want to change on this project. I want to be able to point out this building to my son."

John exemplifies a truth about people leadership: whatever the context we lead in, that context is an opportunity for developing people. For John, building buildings was an opportunity for building people. He understood the importance of people leadership.

People leadership is about bringing out the best in people, and, to do so, leaders focus on three essential functions:

- Selecting the right people and matching them to the right job

- Explaining and clarifying expectations

- Motivating and developing people on the job

Understanding of these functions has been greatly enhanced by research such as the Gallup study described in *First, Break All the Rules* by Marcus Buckingham and Curt Coffman. They provide rich data and detail on what it takes to bring out the best in people, and, although they don't use the term, their focus is on people leadership.

SELECTING THE RIGHT PEOPLE AND MATCHING THEM TO THE RIGHT JOB

Selection is the starting point. If you select the right people, if you match the needs of the job to the skills and talents of the individual, everything else becomes easier. It is easier to explain and clarify expectations, it is easier to motivate your people, and it is easier to develop them.

If you don't select the right people, everything is harder: clarifying, motivating, and developing are harder—and more costly. The problem is not just the direct costs, such as headhunter fees, compensation, training—considerable though they can be. More problematic, and significant, are the indirect costs, such as the time spent by others either covering for deficiencies or trying to instill absent competencies. And more significant still is the cost of lost opportunities, opportunities that would not have been lost had the right person been in the job.

Given the difficulty of fully assessing someone you don't know—someone you are considering bringing in from outside—there is a compelling case for selecting from the inside, especially if you are committed to creating a culture of development (more on that later). Behind the decision to look outside is a misunderstanding about growth and development: many leaders erroneously assume that a person's deficiencies can be trained out and new competencies can be trained in. That is only partially true.

The full truth lies in a helpful distinction that some have made among knowledge, skills, and talents. A person can be given the knowledge required to do something, and, with some discipline, most people can practice something well enough to develop some level of skill; to that extent, training can help. But not everyone has the talent for any given type of work, and talent (or ability) is something inherent. Where talent is evident, gifted leaders of people fan the flame, giving it every opportunity to grow. Where it is latent, they do all they can to expose and ignite it. They don't waste time trying to create talent where talent doesn't exist. As Buckingham and Coffman suggest, "People don't change that much. Don't waste time trying to put in what was left out. Try to draw out what was left in. That is hard enough."

If leaders all understood this, employers would be much more careful about selection processes. They would give selection the time and thought it requires. With the demographic shifts from the baby boomers to Generation X and Generation Y, the talent pool is shrinking and recruitment is likely to become an intense battleground. Selection skills will more than ever become a competitive edge. Great leaders will be great talent spotters.

EXPLAINING AND CLARIFYING EXPECTATIONS

People leadership involves explaining and clarifying expectations. At one level, explaining and clarifying expectations is about delegating, something leaders typically do less well than they think they do. The benefits of delegating are obvious enough. It is good for the person being delegated to: it builds confidence, it communicates trust, it builds ownership, it develops responsibility, and it provides an opportunity for growth and development. It's also good for you as the delegator: it frees you up to concentrate on other priorities, makes you more productive, and relieves stress, not to mention letting you get home earlier.

If the benefits are obvious enough, so are the reasons for the widespread reluctance to delegate. Delegation surfaces real fears: the person may mess up, and the leader will have to clean up the mess. It takes more time to explain what needs to be done than to just do it. And, worst of all, what if, heaven forbid, the employee does a better job than the leader would have done? These objections can easily be countered: mistakes are part of learning, and the leader's job is to support people in the process; it may take time initially, but it saves time in the long run; and selecting people who can do a better job is surely the purpose of good delegation. So, to delegate well, overcome whatever fears you may have and embrace its benefits.

At another level, explaining and clarifying expectations is about *empowerment*—a term widely used and equally widely misused. Empowerment is a function of three components: a clear outcome, sufficient authority and resources, and adequate competence (see Figure 49). The leader's role is to make sure the outcome and the scope are clear, to provide the authority and resources to carry out the assignment, and to make sure that the knowledge and skills—and, even better, the talent—are there to do it.

If you take any one of the three components away, you no longer have empowerment. It's remarkable how often leaders assign a task without giving a clear expectation of the outcome, or how often they assign a task without providing the resources to carry it out, whether time, manpower, or equipment. Insufficient authority is even more damaging; leaders often fail to realize that expectations need to be made clear not only to the person given the responsibility but also to anyone that person will interact with.

Needing explanations and clarification of expectations is also a function of competence. The more competent a person, the less explanation and clarification that person needs; conversely, the less competent, the more explanation is needed.

One of the useful tools in addressing competence was developed by Paul Hersey and Ken Blanchard. *Situational leadership,* as they called it, measures two key ingredients in explaining and clarifying expectations: the amount of direction a person needs and the amount of facilitation that person needs. When you give direction, you tell people what needs to be done. When you facilitate, you open a dialogue; they ask questions, and you answer or ask questions that help

FIGURE 49. THE ELEMENTS OF EMPOWERMENT

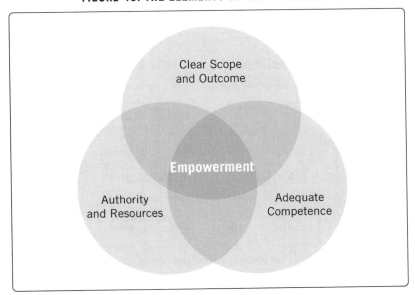

them think through their decisions and actions. Some people need less facilitation and more direction; some need more facilitation and less direction.

You can combine the two concepts to create a grid that reflects a different approach with each combination (see Figure 50).

Depending on the combination, you as a leader act as an instructor, a coach, a facilitator, or a consultant. If you are assigning a new project to an experienced veteran, quadrant four is your best approach. You act as a consultant; they know what to do, and the need for both directive behavior and facilitative behavior is low. If, on the other hand, you are assigning a new project to a young engineer, you will more likely act as a coach, maybe even as an instructor. As people's confidence and competence grow, you will become more facilitative, looking for opportunities to strengthen the skills they are acquiring.

The most frequent and damaging mistake involves micromanaging the competent and giving inadequate clarity and direction to those who need it. Many of us have experienced both. My first real

FIGURE 50. LEVELS OF COMPETENCE

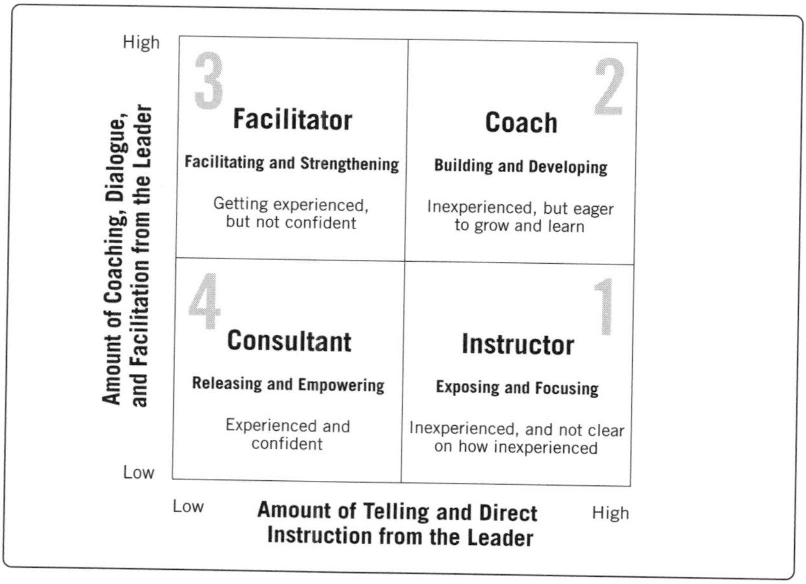

marketplace leadership experience came two years out of college, when I was given the job of supervising a crew of twenty-one people in the dye plant of a British textile manufacturer. The extent of my preparation was being told the time and place to show up. As an employee, I was somewhere in quadrants one or two, but the assignment was given as if I were in quadrant four. With a crew where the average age was fifty-one, and in an environment of acrimonious relationships between the unions and management, I was thrown in at the deep end—and it was by good fortune more than anything else that I managed to gasp enough air between mouthfuls of water to stay reasonably close to the surface! This was followed by another, equally interesting, assignment as production manager for two hundred women making men's underwear. In both cases, the only input I remember was when I had made a mistake. The great benefit of these experiences was that they taught me something of the value of adjusting the way we explain and clarify expectations to the person's level of experience.

MOTIVATING AND DEVELOPING YOUR PEOPLE

Motivating and developing your people is the third essential function of people leadership. To do each part of this function justice, it's necessary to look at them separately.

Motivating Your People

People are free to choose their leaders, so leaders must work to keep their people. Business leaders know that motivated employees stay and their ability to motivate employees helps create situations where they want to stay.

Leaders cannot rely on the weight and authority of their position. Instead, they must lead by influence. Great leaders exercise their influence by appealing to the internal drivers and aspirations of their people, while at the same time providing the external conditions to satisfy those internal aspirations.

Freedom to come and go in the workplace is not the only challenge. People also work in a volatile world where unexpected external events—acts of terrorism, or acts of nature, economic shifts, market changes, and political upheavals—create unexpected pressures and overnight can change people's priorities. Leaders are not only leading a fickle workforce, they are also leading in a volatile workplace.

What does motivate people? How do leaders provide the kind of motivation that keeps people around and also propels them to levels of performance that surprise even themselves?

The leaders who stand out as great motivators are those who address motivation at two levels: an organizational level and an individual level. They provide a motivating climate, and then they stimulate their people to higher levels of performance.

If you have been living out the functions of organizational leadership (creating and clarifying message, aligning the organization and its resources, and selling the direction), as well as the functions of operational leadership (planning and shaping processes, organizing and controlling, and measuring and problem-solving), you have already created a highly motivating environment. Employees know where the organization is going, they know the values are meaningful, they are challenged by the vision, they know how to make their contribution, and they know their efforts will be acknowledged and appreciated. You have set the direction, set the tone, and set up opportunities. You have provided clear leadership. That motivates people.

Some people are particularly gifted in certain aspects of motivation, but much of it is learned. As a leader of people, you can master it by learning five key skills:

- Recognize the different levels of need your people may be facing.

- Line up consequences to support the behaviors you want.

- Distinguish true and false motivators (and focus on the true ones).

- Adjust your approach to the different behavioral styles of your people.

- Provide credible leadership people can trust.

These skills don't all have equal weight. But each plays a role in bringing out the best in your people and bringing them to the point where they perform beyond your or even their own expectations.

Recognize levels of need. Levels of need change. Sometimes people are looking for deep fulfillment; at other times, they're doing their best to survive; and a good leader responds accordingly. Abraham Maslow captured a hierarchy of needs in his five-level pyramid, and Clayton Alderfer captured the same idea with a three-level pyramid (Figure 51). In both, a higher level can't be satisfied unless the lower-level needs have been reasonably satisfied. You can't skip levels—something a good leader recognizes.

Over the years, Maslow's research has been questioned, but the concept makes intuitive sense, and its application to business leaders is most evident when our people are struck by a personal or collective crisis. Under normal circumstances, the natural progression is upward through the pyramid; but, when disaster strikes, whether personal or collective, the direction changes. Someone going through a divorce or worried about their mortgage payments or whether they will have a job after the next round of downsizings may be much less concerned about self-actualization and much more concerned about about meeting physiological and environmental needs. In the wake of a terrorist attack, people suddenly are much less concerned about self-actualization than about self-preservation. Leaders who ignore the shift lose the confidence of their people. So when crises hit, be ready to adjust to an appropriate level of motivational priorities.

FIGURE 51. HIERARCHIES OF PERSONAL NEEDS

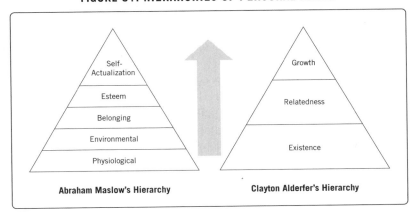

Abraham Maslow's Hierarchy

Self-Actualization
Esteem
Belonging
Environmental
Physiological

Clayton Alderfer's Hierarchy

Growth
Relatedness
Existence

Line up consequences to support behaviors. Focusing on the direct relationship between behaviors (inputs) and consequences (outcomes) takes the discussion a notch higher. With this approach, you motivate people by defining the behaviors you want and shaping the outcomes to provide the consequences most likely to generate those behaviors. Parents swear by this approach ("If you don't eat your vegetables, you can't have dessert"). Managers motivate using the same approach ("If you do this, you'll get that").

This behaviorist approach to motivation is well represented by proponents such as Aubrey Daniels, who looked at consequences from three perspectives:

- Is the consequence positive or negative?

- Is the consequence immediate or future?

- Is the consequence certain or uncertain?

In each case, one is preferable to the other: the consequence needs to be positive rather than negative, immediate rather than future, and certain rather than uncertain.

If you want to release initiative and creativity, you need positive consequences. Negative consequences typically only motivate to the level that avoids the negative consequence, and no higher. However, negative consequences are appropriate when you need to define clear boundaries. Deferred consequences are less motivating than immediate consequences, whether tangible (such as money) or intangible (such as praise or recognition).

Uncertain consequences are also weak motivators. If something might or might not happen, people are more likely to do whatever they want. Why do some employees resist wearing safety glasses? Why do some incentive programs raise no interest? Often because the consequences are uncertain.

This approach to motivation works well for quantifiable behavior—increasing the number of sales calls per hour, or the amount of concrete poured on a job site in a given time frame, or the productivity of a piece of equipment. The less quantifiable the behavior, the harder it is to apply an appropriate consequence and thus motivate the desired behavior. We are, after all, also morally motivated beings; our moral choices may not include a weighing of consequences or even align with our—or our leader's—self-interest.

Distinguish true and false motivators. Much of the confusion over motivation comes from the failure to distinguish between those elements that appear to be motivators but in fact aren't, and those elements that may not seem significant but in reality are.

Back in the 1960s, Frederick Herzberg made the helpful distinction between hygiene factors and motivators (first published in *Harvard Business Review* in 1968). *Hygiene factors*—a curious term that refers figuratively to the overall health of an organization's climate—are those factors that if properly addressed reduce dissatisfaction, but in themselves don't motivate. They simply improve working conditions without improving productivity. They include adjusting company policies and administrative procedures, raising salaries, and improving working conditions. Having a low salary or poor physical working conditions is a dissatisfier, but improving either one is not a motivator. It simply removes the dissatisfaction. In other words, satisfaction and motivation are not the same.

The *motivators* are less tangible but more powerful—a sense of achievement and accomplishment, recognition and appreciation for good performance, the nature of the work itself, increased responsibility, advancement and promotion, opportunities for growth, and so on—than the satisfiers.

The ability to distinguish satisfiers from motivators separates great leaders from the rest. Even today, more than thirty years after Herzberg's research, leaders still confuse satisfiers and motivators and assume that money, working conditions, and a generous benefits package are the primary motivators. They underestimate the impact of recognition and well-timed, well-placed praise, and the inherent motivation derived from a job the person enjoys and is well suited to.

The cost of using real motivators is low, and the impact is high. When you write a short thank-you note of appreciation for a great effort and a great performance, there's not much likelihood that the recipient will throw it away. People are likely to treasure such notes for years.

Great leaders don't ignore the dissatisfiers. If they can address them, they do. They just don't expect that removing them will deliver the same results as providing genuine motivators.

Adjust your approach to different behavioral styles. I have been addressing motivation in general terms—how people in general are motivated. But it's important to recognize that different people are mo-tivated differently. The past thirty years have seen a greater interest in the individual dimension of motivation, which has built on the more general earlier conclusions.

Much of this interest began in the 1940s when a mother-daughter team took Carl Jung's work and developed the Myers-Briggs® assessment of individual preferences. It continued in the 1950s, as researchers like David Merrill and William Marston focused on behavioral styles, culminating in the first version of the DiSC® instrument developed by John Geier in 1969, becoming the inspiration for other instruments developed over subsequent decades.

The great contribution of such instruments has been to underscore the point that effective motivation is highly individualized and personalized. Most of these approaches are based on David Merrill's intersection of two scales: responsiveness and assertiveness. Responsiveness is driven either by a task focus or a people focus; assertiveness is geared toward either initiating or supporting. When you intersect these two you get very different and often conflicting motivations: the incentives for someone motivated by task will differ from the incentives for someone motivated by people, and those motivated by initiating change in the status quo will respond differently from those intent on supporting its preservation. The clear implication for a leader is that to motivate people effectively, you have to know them and tailor your efforts to the drivers of their particular behavioral style. It's difficult to motivate well without being a student of your people.

Provide credible leadership. If the discussion stopped here, you might come away with the conclusion that motivation is primarily a function of having the right information and applying the right techniques. Address the right level, apply the appropriate consequence, focus on motivators rather than satisfiers, adjust to behavioral styles— and you have a motivated workforce.

It isn't quite that simple.

Everything I've said thus far matters little if you do not have the trust of your people. You can try to understand them, adjust to their behavioral style, recognize their level of need, and place them in the job that matches their talents; but, if they don't trust you, they will see every effort as manipulation. In times of economic hardship, your credibility is more important than ever. It's more important than any charisma, charm, and persuasiveness.

So keep communication open. Keep your word. Tell people everything you know; if you don't know, tell them you will find out. If you know and can't tell them, tell them you can't tell them, and tell them why. Guard your integrity, for on it stands or falls your credibility—as well as your ability to motivate your people when everything is conspiring to sap that motivation.

If you know how to motivate people, you will be a leader in high demand. If you don't know how, these are skills you can learn. Once you do, you will have found the way to greater levels of satisfaction for the people you are leading and, at the same time, to increased profitability, retention rates, productivity, creativity, and customer satisfaction for your organization. Not a bad payoff for learning a new skill.

Developing Your People

Development is a powerful motivator. If you help someone move from poor to average, from average to good, and from good to great, you have released the internal energy of a highly motivated individual. If you help uncover and exercise talents their possessor wasn't aware of, you also earn that person's lifelong gratitude.

Like motivation, people development has two dimensions, organizational and individual. Its primary focus is on the individual, but that focus is reinforced by a corporate climate that values and encourages the individual investment development requires.

Development is about focus. It's about distance. It's about involvement. You can't develop people without focusing on and getting involved with them individually. But development also needs planning and purpose. Effective development is

- *Planned:* It isn't haphazard; thought goes into it.

- *Purpose-Driven:* It's tied to the purposes of the organization.

- *Personal:* It's customized to the needs of the individual.

One of the characteristics that marks the military is its commitment to the intentional development of its leaders. And for good reason: the military has no choice; it can't go and raid the corporate world when it's short of senior leaders. That reality is an asset, because it results in a very intentional approach to leadership development.

Military personnel use a deceptively simple approach. Before they carry out an assignment, they spend plenty of time preparing for it, and after they have been through the assignment, they spend plenty of time reviewing it. Often the time spent in preparation and feedback seems disproportionate: a flight mission of one to two hours may be wedged in between several hours of preparation and feedback on either side. The preparation helps, but so does the anticipation of feedback at the other end, which sharpens a person's concentration during the assignment. The feedback not only provides input, it also provides accountability.

Start looking for the opportunities to apply this cycle of preparation, assignment, and feedback. It's surprising how many you will find. It's like buying a new car—once you decide which make and model you want, you start seeing that car all over the place. Have more of them suddenly appeared? No—your decision has just made you more aware of them. So it is with development: your decision to develop people opens your eyes to opportunities you didn't see before. When you visit a client, you think about who could benefit from the experience of going with you. If you are preparing a budget, you ask yourself who could benefit by learning how to do it. Anything you currently do can become a development opportunity.

This cycle of preparation, assignment, and feedback (see Figure 52) is powerful. It works best when the culture reinforces the cycle, just as the military does. The more highly development is valued in the culture, the more likely the leaders are to be intimately engaged in the cycle.

Over the past two decades, coaching has become a widely accepted practice in the marketplace, a further validation of investment in one-on-one development. Coaching conjures up varied images,

FIGURE 52. INDIVIDUAL DEVELOPMENT CYCLE

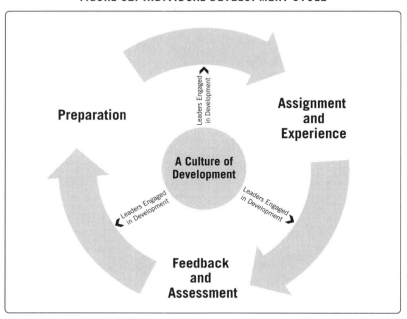

from the tantrums of a Bobby Knight to the serene composure of a John Wooden. The desirable image is a focus on uncovering the aspirations and talents of individuals and placing them in the context that will best nurture those talents. "Today's leader," writes James Belasco, "is a people-developer and relationship-builder who asks, 'How can I help this person become more valuable as an individual as well as to all of us?' Today's leader is a coach."

Like anything with a high yield, coaching requires a high investment, and you may be wondering whether the investment is worth it. It is, on three counts: what it does for the organization, what it does for the person being developed, and what it does for you, the developer.

The organization benefits. Research is delivering some compelling data. Several studies suggest returns on investment of up to 788 percent—which leads many organizations to the conclusion that, not only can they afford to make the investment, they cannot afford not to. The 788 percent figure is from results posted by MetrixGlobal on

Nortel Networks. The *Manchester Review* recently published the results of a study suggesting an ROI of 570 percent. (For a more complete review of research data on the benefits of coaching, see *FMI Quarterly*, 2003, Issue 2, "Coaching Organizational Players.") Research has also revealed a multiplying effect: when people have benefited from a leader investing in their development, they are more likely, in turn, to make a similar investment in someone else. Noel Tichy's research reported in *The Leadership Engine* (2002) bears this out:

> In winning companies, leading and teaching are considered so essential to success that they aren't reserved for a favored few in the executive suite. Winning companies know that games are won and lost on the playing field, and victory goes to the team with the most good players. So they nurture, and expect, leadership everywhere. In winning companies, teaching, learning and leading are inherent parts of everyone's job description.

The individual benefits. Benefits to the individual are obvious and intuitive, but the research documents gains in productivity and much more. Organizations that invest in coaching are noting improved relationships with direct reports, improved relationships with stakeholders, improved teamwork, improved relationships with peers, improved job satisfaction, reduced conflict, increased organizational commitment, and improved relationships with clients.

You, the leader, benefit. Your investment in developing others pays some significant dividends:

- *You put your career on a different footing.* Professional success is an elusive concept, but it is ultimately defined by the ability to make other people successful. This shifts your focus from creating your own success to creating other people's success, and that shift actually enhances your career. It helps to focus on impact, not on promotion, and when you do, promotion takes care of itself. You become a talent developer, someone who has learned how to nurture talent to its full potential.

- *You'll get your time back.* Although making this investment requires time, the rewards come back in exponential timesaving. In the long run, the time you save is in proportion to the time you invest in developing others.

■ *You will become an accomplished talent spotter.* There is a direct correlation between talent development and talent spotting: the more skilled you become at developing talent, the more easily you recognize it.

■ *Your reputation will be built on more than just competence.* In the past, a reputation for getting work done may have been good enough, and it may not have mattered how. But today's marketplace is different; getting the job done is still important, but how you get the job done is equally important. Character does matter, and developing people builds a reputation for character because it focuses on how you help other people become successful—a key ingredient of character.

■ *You will build a lasting network of relationships.* Remember the truism that success depends on who you know? By becoming a respected developer of people, you gain the support and respect not only of an organization grateful for your investment in its future, but also of the people in whose lives you have invested. Loyalty is hard to come by, but a great way of earning it is to hone your skills as a developer of people.

■ *You will leave a legacy.* Even if your organization is not committed to creating a culture of development, you will be contributing to the one key factor that more than any other will shape the future of the company—the quality and caliber of its future leaders. Every project you engage in, every building you build, every contact you make, and every initiative you undertake is an opportunity to develop someone who, with your guidance, could become a builder of the organization's future greatness.

■ *You will keep growing.* Leaders are learners, and investing in others keeps you learning. "If I want to learn something, I teach it," Ken Blanchard once said. You could just as easily say, "If I want to grow, I invest in others." Doing so keeps leaders from settling into the comfort of their entrenched assumptions, it helps them confront their blind spots. You are less likely to get derailed because investing in others keeps you fresh, receptive, and connected.

So why should you invest in others? What's in it for you? Plenty! Enduring success based on what really counts, a deep sense of fulfillment and contribution, and a strong legacy and lasting impact, along with a solid reputation among your leaders, peers, and direct reports and a lasting network of friends. As a return on investment, that's pretty hard to beat.

CONCLUSION

Your Leadership Development Curriculum

"Some men are born great," Shakespeare tells us, "some achieve greatness, and some have greatness thrust upon them."

Shakespeare had it right—we can achieve greatness. You may be one of the few, the very few, who are born great. If you are, however, a mere mortal like the rest of us, greatness is still within your grasp.

If there is anything this book set out to accomplish, it is to give you the tools and the confidence to achieve greatness. Its purpose has been to give you a framework to think and act your way to great leadership, bringing sense to its complexity, making leadership "as simple as possible," in the words of Einstein, "and no simpler."

This book, then, can serve as a curriculum for your personal development as a leader. Achieving greatness doesn't just happen. It requires intentionality, and this book can help you bring structure to your intentions.

Great leadership requires both character and competence. Which of these resonated the most with you?

If it was character, was it the notion of a personal philosophy of leadership? If it was, start collecting in a notebook your thoughts on what drives and frames great leadership. Collect your thoughts on the source of your authority, bring definition to your view of human nature, clarify your sense of purpose and destiny—all three key concepts in defining your philosophy of leadership. Was it the notion of self-awareness and the need for feedback? If it was, consider how to glean the invaluable feedback that can only raise the level of your effectiveness as a leader. Use some of the suggestions at the end of Chapter 4 to guide your actions.

Was it one of the building blocks in the pyramid of personal qualities that struck a chord? If it was, identify people, past or present, who exemplify it, and consider how to emulate them. Which of the three core building blocks—humility, focus, and care for others—evoked your strongest response? Perhaps it was one of the qualities generated by the core building blocks. If it was, consider how that quality applies to the leadership challenges you face.

If it was competence that resonated with you, was it the interplay between organizational leadership and operational leadership? If it was, identify where your current role is on the face of the Leadership Cube; identify also where the roles you aspire to are on the face of the cube. Consider the three essential functions of each one and how they apply to your particular leadership role. Review Chapter 6, "The Three Dimensions of Leadership," and find the touch points in Mike's story that connect with your circumstances. If your promotions have been steady and consistent, consider how well your adjustment from operational leadership to organizational leadership has been keeping pace with your promotions.

If the competence issue that most spoke to you was people leadership, which of the three functions spoke the loudest? Was it selecting and matching the right person to the right job? Was it explaining and clarifying expectations? Consider how each applies to your current role. Was it motivating your people? If it was, consider which element of motivation needs strengthening. Was it developing your people? If it was, start looking for ways to apply the development cycle.

Become a student of great leadership. It doesn't matter where you start. Let your intuition guide you as you move around the framework; it will show you what strengths to build and what gaps to fill. If you haven't already, develop a taste for reading, and focus your reading on your personal curriculum. Leaders are readers.

Become not just a student of great leadership but also a teacher of great leadership. Whatever you're learning, pass it on. And with the same intentionality you apply to your development as a leader, use this framework to shape the curriculum that best serves the leadership development of those directly or indirectly in your charge. Ask them the same questions you asked yourself—the questions raised in the preceding paragraphs—and guide them as they work through their curriculum.

A final word. Inevitably our leadership is tested, and that's when we "have greatness thrust upon us"—whether we want it or not. In *The Lord of the Rings*, Frodo, the unlikely hero entrusted with the task of disposing of the ring, laments to Gandalf, "I wish the ring had never come to me. I wish none of this had happened." In response, the ever-wise Gandalf replies, "So do all who live to see such times. But that is not for them to decide. All we have to decide is what to do with the time that is given to us."

Deciding what to do with the time that is given to us is much easier if we have fashioned and followed a curriculum that guides our growth as a leader. You may not be a Washington facing a war for independence, a Lincoln facing a civil war, or a Churchill facing a world war, but times will come when you face battles. That's when the curriculum will have served you well, because when greatness is thrust upon you, you will be equipped to embrace it. That's when you will know that greatness is indeed within your grasp.

ABOUT THE AUTHOR

Antony Bell is president and CEO of Leader Development, Inc., a leadership and organization development firm whose purpose is to provide the framework and relationships that enable leaders to understand, exercise, and teach great leadership. The company's leadership development specialists have extensive leadership experience and strong academic credentials, and include former CEOs and senior corporate executives, PhDs, psychologists, and senior military officers. Leader Development, Inc., is recognized for its ability to help organizations engage in significant change, for the quality and effectiveness of its executive team development, and for the quality of its executive coaching.

Bell grew up in France and Great Britain, and his professional and executive experience spans the United Kingdom, France, Germany, Switzerland, the Netherlands, South Africa, and the United States. He earned his bachelor's degree in business and economics in the United Kingdom and his master's degree in European law and business institutions in France. Over the years, he has worked with hundreds of professional leaders—all looking for a path to greatness in leadership. He and his wife, Betsy, currently make their home in Columbia, South Carolina.

For more information on Leader Development, Inc., or on Antony Bell as a speaker, please visit www.leaderdevelopmentinc.com or call 803-748-1005.

INDEX

ability to act, 80–81
ability to laugh at oneself, 89
ability to think, 78–80
absolutes, 56, 60
Ackman, Fred, 71–72
Adams, Abigail, 7, 41
Adams, John, 18–19, 22, 41–42
Adizes, Ichak, 117
Albrecht, Karl, 112, 132
Alderfer, Clayton, 188–89
alignment: organizational, 117, 152; process, 178
Allen, Richard, 88
American business: Japan's infiltration into, 23; management's role in, 21
American Revolution, 18–19, 60
analysis, 177–78
Aristotle, 36, 80
arrogance, 74–75
assertiveness, 191
Auden, W. H., 89
audiences, 153–54
authenticity: self-awareness and, 62; substance and, 88
authority, 55–57
autocracy, 116–17

bad leadership, 38
Bates, Edward, 85
behaviors: consequences to support, 189–90; driving factors, 63, 65; intentional pattern of, 67; leadership-related, 52–53; personality expressed in, 64; talents

expressed in, 64; unconscious formation of, 51–52; values' effect on, 148
Belasco, James, 194
Bennis, Warren, 24–25
Berwick, Don, 125
big hairy audacious goals, 141
Blanchard, Ken, 26, 184, 196
Bonhoeffer, Dietrich, 60
Bossidy, Larry, 39, 172, 176–77
Buckingham, Marcus, 182–83
business literature, 14–15
business performance, 4–5
business process reengineering, 27, 172

Capone, Al, 43
care for others: description of, 42, 81; sacrifice for others and, 81–82
Carter, Jimmy, 24
change: description of, 13; elements of, 128; equation for, 157–58; managing of, 154–58; perceptions of, 156; resistance to, 155–57; speed of, 13; stages of, 155–56. *See also* organizational change
change agents, 154, 156
character: absence of, 39–40; competence and, 35–38, 46–47, 109; culture as, 122; definition of, 39; description of, 30, 33–34, 199–200; importance of, 37, 47; noble ends and, 39–40, 61; noble